September 2017
To Denny [illegible]
Best Wishes
[illegible]

Fighting Bob

Bob Stockton

authorHOUSE®

AuthorHouse™
1663 Liberty Drive
Bloomington, IN 47403
www.authorhouse.com
Phone: 1-800-839-8640

First published by AuthorHouse 7/13/2011

ISBN: 978-1-4634-3072-6 (sc)
ISBN: 978-1-4634-3073-3 (hc)
ISBN: 978-1-4634-3074-0 (e)

Library of Congress Control Number: 2011911127

Printed in the United States of America

–also by Bob Stockton–

Listening To Ghosts

'Fighting Bob' is dedicated to all who have sailed in a fast ship into harm's way.

Contents

CHAPTER ONE

It was while I was recovering from a particularly nasty motorcycle accident last year that I decided to write the book. I had been threatening to put pen to paper and write an autobiography that would chronicle my many adventures and mishaps during a twenty year Navy career but had never done anything about it. The project would be just the ticket to keep me busy while all these broken ribs and sundry other bumps and bruises healed. I would begin the next day by requesting a copy of my Navy Service Record from the Military Record Archives in Saint Louis. Those papers would clear up some of the fuzziness surrounding the dates and locations of my service that had begun more than half a century earlier.

The next afternoon I printed and filled out the online form requesting the documents, put them in an envelope and dropped the request in the mailbox, returning with a sense of accomplishment that I was finally getting the ball rolling on the damn book that I had promised to many but had never written.

Late afternoon had arrived and a November chill was in the air. The pain from the five broken ribs was pretty intense so I made a sandwich, took a couple of prescription pain pills, applied a new Fentanyl patch and settled gingerly into the upright recliner that would become my bed for the next several months. Relief from the all-consuming pain could not come quickly enough. Maybe a gin and tonic on top of the meds would hasten the relief. I got up slowly and headed for the Bombay bottle in the kitchen, thinking all the while about the pain and suffering I wanted to inflict on the idiot that ran the red light a week ago and put me in the emergency room.

I mixed the Bombay and tonic - a little heavy on the Bombay side of the equation - and returned to the recliner to wait for the meds and the booze to kick in, which did not take long at all. The house was dark and a bit cool and I felt a wave of relief rescue me from the ever present pain.

I was drifting in and out of a fuzzy sleep when out of the corner of my eye I thought I saw some movement by the hallway. I could swear I saw the shadow of someone moving silently about the house. I knew that I was alone, my son had left over an hour ago and I was not expecting anyone to arrive. Was I hallucinating or was there really someone else in the house with me?

"Adam, is that you?" I could hear myself speaking but my voice seemed to come from outside my body, from another part of the house. I remember thinking that the Fentanyl patch was *really* cooking! I made a mental note not to mix gin and pain patches in the future.

No answer.

"Adam, goddammit this isn't funny. What are you still doing here? I thought you left."

Still no answer. The sound of my voice was still distant from my body. Out of the corner of my eye I saw a shadowy ghost-like figure move swiftly across the room.

"Who are you and what are you doing here?" The sound of my voice sounded as if it were coming from the next room. "What do you want?"

Still no answer. Obviously, there is no one here, I thought. Just the damn Fentanyl and gin causing some disorientation in my mind. Yet I had the distinct sensation that I was in the presence of some being, some entity living or otherwise whose presence in the house was unmistakable even though I could not actually see or touch whoever or whatever it was. I remember thinking that I ought to be afraid but somehow I was not. Curious? Yes. Afraid? Not at all. Whether it was the booze, the pills, the patch, or perhaps some other manifestation of my mind designed to help me forget about the pain I knew that there was no danger.

"Do you not know who I am, Robert?"

Whatever this thing was had a back channel directly into my brain. The voice was like a thought in my mind.

Weirdness!

"Well, no I don't know who you are but I suspect that you are inside my head courtesy of the pain meds I'm taking to help with these damn broken ribs." I remember thinking that I hadn't been called *Robert* in that authoritative tone of voice in many years, a voice that was usually reserved for my dead grandmother to use when I was in trouble for having broken some rule or dodged some chore but the 'voice' was that of a man, a man used to getting his way.

Might as well go with the flow, I remember thinking, and see where this all ends up, probably in a detox center somewhere.

"Close your eyes and concentrate, sir. What do you see?"

I closed my eyes as the thing asked - commanded was more like it - and tried to focus on the sound of the voice that I was hearing. At first, I could see nothing but blackness but after a bit I began to discern a rather indistinct apparition, hazy and ill defined.

I must be hallucinating, I thought.

"WHAT DO YOU SEE, MAN? SPEAK UP."

This thing was obviously used to getting its way, and yet for some reason I had no fear of it.

"Well, whoever or whatever you are, you appear to be a man in his mid forties with a set of mutton chops and curly hair that hides a widow's peak. You are wearing a uniform of some kind, probably that of a Navy Officer of the mid nineteenth century. Although you have not fully beamed up to me here, I think that we must be related somehow. You are a Stockton, but I can't be sure exactly which one."

"Very well, sir, as far as it goes. I believe that if you have your wits about you determining 'which one' as you so casually describe

me should be within your grasp. And just what exactly does your phrase 'fully beamed up' signify?"

"Beaming up was a phrase on a television program that described molecular dispersion of.... Well, anyway I meant it to describe the fact that your image is not altogether clear and distinct in my mind. As to which relative of mine, seeing as Pop's family were mostly Army officers and lawyers I'll take an educated guess that you are Commodore Stockton."

"Well done, sir. I am in fact the Commodore and am also your great-great-great grandfather."

"Pleased to meet you, sort of, Commodore. I suppose that there is a valid reason for this hallucinatory visit, but I have no idea what that reason would be, and quite frankly were the choice of hallucinations my own I'd have selected a much more entertaining one of the opposite gender."

Old Grandpop had not been in the room more than ten minutes and already I was beginning to sound like the pompous old martinet.

"Hold your tongue, sir. Impertinence toward senior officers is not befitting a Stockton junior."

I had forgotten that our so-called 'conversation' was strictly inside my head. The old Commodore could 'hear' my every thought.

"And what is more you shall address me as 'Commodore' when we converse. Familial ties have no bearing on the upcoming exchanges that we will have. I am a Naval Commodore, commander of fighting

ships of the line, conqueror of the Mexican territory of California and the first Governor of that territory. I have successfully fought Barbary pirates and the British, defeated the Mexican Generals Castro and Flores and have won numerous duels. I have served as a United States Senator and was once considered a potential presidential nominee. Great-great-great grandson or no, you will address me in a manner as befits my naval rank."

"What the hell. Commodore it is then. Stocktons have never been known to me to be terribly attached to extended family ties anyway. Is there a reason for this visit? I mean, why are you here?"

"Commodore? Commodore?"

No answer.

Whatever it was had left the building. Apparently, what was transpiring was going to be all about him and I had a feeling that the old Commodore was going to be with me again. I gingerly shifted my position in the recliner and dropped of into a restless sleep.

It was close to midnight when the pain woke me up. The house had gotten very cold. I eased up out of the recliner - even bringing it to the upright position was painful - and shuffled off to the bedroom to retrieve my old horse blanket bathrobe and the comforter on the bed. The damn bed looked *so* inviting but I knew better than to try to lay down on it. The doc had warned me that my rib cage would not allow it. After several attempts I got the robe around me, grabbed the comforter and headed back to the recliner in the living room.

It was time to apply another Fentanyl patch.

As I unwrapped the patch, I suddenly remembered the dream about the Commodore that I had dreamt earlier that evening. It had seemed so real that I almost believed that the encounter with the Commodore had actually happened, that it had occurred exactly as I have described here. Of course, I knew that I had not actually been having a conversation with a relative who had been dead for almost 150 years, but damn! It felt so damn real!

Patch applied, I threw together a peanut butter and jelly sandwich - I had learned the hard way not to use the patch on an empty stomach, popped two pain pills and just for the hell of it mixed another Bombay and tonic, being careful not to lean too heavily on the gin and returned to the recliner I waited for the meds to kick in which surprisingly didn't take all that long.

Sweet relief. Maybe this will hold me until tomorrow. I could feel myself again melting away into a state of blissful somnolence.

"I believe that we were in the middle of a conversation when you so unceremoniously left the room. I must tell you sir, that I consider that to be an affront and were we not of family I would be forced to offer a duel to satisfy this indignity."

"I.........I left the.......wait...........wait a minute," I was trying to clear my head from the fog that the pain meds had induced.

"Look, Commodore, or Granddad, or Bob, or Senator or

whatever you wish to be called, lets tidy this up a bit. In the first place, I am dreaming this and you are not a real entity. You have been dead for what, some 150 years? Secondly, I *am* your great-great-great grandson and not some junior rating under your command and as such I suggest that we speak as adult men. Finally, just why am I dreaming this? What is the reason for this visit, if this is a visit and not some hallucination?"

The silence was deafening.

After a lengthy pause the apparition replied softly:

"Such impertinence. Very well, Grandson. I shall call you Robert. You may continue to address me as Commodore."

"As for my being an actual entity, I can assure you that your experience this day is ***very*** *real. You are visiting me in* ***my*** *domain, although I cannot say exactly what mechanism has caused this. However, the mechanism itself is of little import. I have a mission for you to undertake."*

A mission. What sort of mission could this long dead relative have for me, and for that matter why me?

"I have chosen you for this mission.....

I had forgotten that the Commodore could 'hear' my thoughts.

".....because you are most suited to complete that which I require. Your generation has had little experience with Naval Service and the generations immediately preceding yours have all been army officers, politicians or lawyers and have little more than a

landlubbers acquaintance of a life at sea. No, Robert, you are best suited for this charge, although I daresay that had you applied yourself in a more serious manner you could have been more useful to both yourself and your twenty years of Naval service."

Praise with faint damns. Or was it the other way around?

"Commodore, as you can see - if that is the appropriate verb - I am recovering from an accident that has broken five of my ribs on my 'starboard' side, along with several other contusions and may be out of commission for months. I am not sure that I can be of much help to you in my current state. Even if I were healthy I doubt that I would have the qualifications for this 'task' that you would like me to do for you."

"Nonsense, Robert. You are perfectly capable of executing this task. I want you to write a book. You are already contemplating writing your memoirs so you obviously have the skills necessary to chronicle my contributions to our great country."

So there it was. Old Granddad - enough of all these 'great-greats' - wanted me to chronicle his place in history, as if there had not been enough already written about the old.....

"Have a care, sir. Choose your words. Wisely."

This inside the head thing was getting to be tiresome.

"Fine, Granddad. I assume that this will be a sort of oral history of your exploits as told to me by you. If nothing else, it will be fascinating to hear of your exploits out west. I don't know much about writing history so I'll probably write this in the form of a novel."

"I do not object to that. The public will derive great pleasure when they read your accounting of my naval career. You will achieve great fame and notoriety."

"Well sir, I don't know about the fame and notoriety part, but it should be a lot of fun putting this together. I'll do it."

"There are times when you twenty-first century Americans affect the ***strangest*** *pattern of speech. We will continue at our next encounter."*

And he was gone.

I was beginning to detect a pattern in the Commodore's visits with me. They were occurring between sunset and sunrise and seemed always to break off when my pain medication was on the wane. When I took another dose of the meds (augmented with a sip or two of the juniper berry) I could expect another visit from the old gentleman. My guess is that the narcotic effect on my brain had somehow 'unlocked' a part of my subconscious that gave the Commodore access.

Alternatively, perhaps the 'cocktail' of drugs and booze had opened some vault deep in the recesses of my brain where the Commodore and God knows who or what else resided..

Either way the whole thing was kind of exciting!

CHAPTER TWO

Several days had passed since I last had a 'visit' from the Commodore. I was reasonably certain that the whole experience had been nothing more than a drug induced dream and not a visit from the beyond from old Granddad. In a way I was somewhat sorry that the whole affair had just been a figment of my imagination. I was beginning to enjoy the back and forth between what was probably one part of my narcotic soaked brain and another. Maybe this is how one comes to be dependent on these painkillers, I thought. I had briefly considered cutting back or discontinuing some of the meds but the pain was more intense than ever. I decided that it was too soon to wean myself from the drugs.

It was early evening of the fourth day of my return from the hospital. Time for another dose. I made a sandwich, replaced the old patch, took two more pain pills and poured myself a Bombay and Tonic and headed for the recliner - the damn thing was beginning to feel more like the rack - and eased myself ever so carefully into the seat. Maybe tonight would be the night that I would be able to get a couple of hours of real sleep.

Whoosh! That patch really grabs hold. Mmh.

"Robert. Robert. Focus on me. We have work to do."

"Commodore. Where have you been the last couple of days?"

I was amazed to find that I was glad to 'see' the old buzzard again.

The Commodore was silent for a moment or two and then heaved an exasperated sigh.

"Old buzzard, sir? May I remind you that you are seeing me as I was in the time of the war with Mexico, an apparition that is some twenty years younger than you sitting there in that contraption feeling sorry for yourself. May I also remind you of your duty to respect my former position as Naval Commodore and your ancestor."

"Sorry."

"Let's see now, you want me to write some sort of journal that will describe your contributions to the building of our country. I have to say that I am really jazzed - excited - about doing this. All I know about you is that you have a city in California named for you."

"Yes. Well then let us begin at the time I entered The College of New Jersey - I believe that it has since been renamed Princeton University - in the year 1808 at the age of thirteen. My father Richard who was commonly known as 'The Old Duke' was a lawyer of some great renown and the son of Richard Stockton who affixed his name to the document which declared our country's independence from the British oppression. Our home in Princeton

was built on a large tract of land purchased from William Penn long before our war for independence."

I had to interject: "Thirteen? You enrolled in college when you were thirteen?"

"That is correct. Please be so kind as to not interrupt while I am speaking."

"As I was saying, I enrolled in the College of New Jersey at thirteen and I must say that I excelled in the academic application of mathematics, languages and engineering . My father, the Old Duke had high hopes for me to stand for the Bar and receive my law degree, but I must confess that I had a strong desire for adventure and the smell of salt air and gunpowder. Yet another war with John Bull was looming on the horizon and I yearned for action; the ennui and tedium of the classroom was stifling. There would be no reading at the Bar for me. It was the lure of adventure on the high seas that held sway over me."

"The exploits of Lord Nelson had been heralded with great favor among our society and being a high spirited lad I prevailed upon my father to procure for me a midshipman's warrant, receiving same in the late summer of 1811. I was fifteen years and eleven months of age."

"Lord Nelson? I would think that you would have wanted someone to emulate like our own John Paul Jones. After all, he was a great American naval hero. Why Nelson?"

"Lord Nelson was the most remarkable of men. He died a hero's death in battle whereas Captain Jones, after achieving great notoriety in his naval engagements, sold his service as a mercenary

to a Russian Empress. It was looked upon with great disfavor at the time. Lord Nelson's doctrine of 'creative disobedience' while fraught with danger and the possibility of calamitous outcome served him well in his naval engagements. Indeed, in my later years when I commanded ships of the line I often employed his philosophy, achieving many successes."

"Creative disobedience? What the hell does that mean?"

"Simply put sir, creative disobedience allows the subordinate commander to seize the opportunity for victory over one's adversary through independent action even if the maneuver taken is contrary to the standing orders of the naval senior present in the engagement. But the forehanded maneuver had best result in victory or the junior is sure to be court martialed and perhaps cashiered."

"I can see where the concept got its name. A calculated risk. I doubt whether today's commanders would be that daring."

"Be that as it may the doctrine essentially prioritizes the ultimate goal in wartime: Do we wish to defeat our enemy or are we merely to blindly follow the written orders of a senior when that senior has no firsthand knowledge of the immediate tactical situation. Do we choose action or lockstep? I for one choose action."

"The subordinate commander must be prepared to stand by his actions even in the face of courts-martial. I recall the year 1821 during my first command when I encountered such a difficulty."

This ought to be good. "What happened, Granddad?"

"Well sir, I had applied to Secretary of the Navy Thomson for a command. As I recall my exact words were along the order of 'a

command of the most dangerous, difficult and uncompromising employment at the disposal of our government.' I had previously applied for command to no avail but this request was granted. I received orders to the Boston Navy Yard to assume command of the schooner **Alligator** *which was under construction there. Captain Isaac Hull was the Commandant of the Navy Yard and my orders were to report to him."*

"The **USS Alligator.** What type of ship was she?"

"Alligator *was a schooner, much like the British privateers that played such havoc with our Navy during the 1812 conflict. She was fast, sleek, displaced 200 tons and carried 12 six pounders. She was manned by a crew of seventy of the finest sailors in our young fleet."*

"Six pounders?" Another sigh issued from the Commodore.

"A six pounder was a naval cannon mounted on a wheeled carriage that fired six pound lead shot. If you please sir, may I be allowed to continue?"

"By all means, Commodore. Please resume your enthralling narrative."

I wondered if the old gent was as keen on sarcasm as he was on retelling his adventures.

"I had received strong sponsorship from members of the 'Colonization Society,' a group of influential Americans who had prevailed upon Presidents Jefferson and later Monroe to assist in the establishment of a colony in western Africa where freed American slaves could be transported to create their own society. Secretary Thomson,

after much urging from Supreme Court Justice Washington - who happened to be a close friend of the Old Duke - drafted orders to despatch the **Alligator** *to suppress the active slave trade in those volatile waters. My orders also directed me to make contact with the United States Agents there who were engaged in finding a suitable locale for such a freed slave colony."*

"So our policy was one of righting the moral wrong of slavery in America?"

"Would that that were so, but no. The reality of the situation was that slave owners feared that the freed slaves in America would foment uprisings among their plantation slaves. This had happened earlier in the century in Virginia when a freed slave by the name of Prosser's Gabriel had instigated a short lived uprising. After that aborted attempt slave owners were searching for the 'humane' disposition of freed slaves to a colony in western Africa."

"What happened to Prosser?"

"He was hanged along with some twenty-odd of his followers. Please try to hold your interruptions to a minimum, Robert."

"No offense meant. It is just that I tend to want to know some of your story in a bit more detail. Kind of interesting to me. Please go ahead."

"The actual reading of my orders directed me to interdict only American ships engaged in the slave trade, but the reality of the on scene situation was that most slavers carried more than one national flag to run up the yardarm. If an American slaver detected our presence she had merely to hoist the flag of a foreign nation which would then protect her from boarding and prize taking."

"In that case you must have had a pretty dull cruise. I remember a time in 1958 when our destroyer was sent southeast of French Frigate Shoals to wait for......"

"Robert, please remain focused on my narrative. I sense that our time for this meeting is growing short."

"The point of this chronological diversion is to demonstrate my adoption of Nelson's 'creative disobedience' strategy. My superiors were more than four thousand nautical miles removed from the scene. I was not to be dissuaded from my duty to interdict slave traders and free the captured slaves. I was not an advocate for trafficking in human misery. Foreign flag or no, I would defeat the traders in battle and take their vessels as prize. Within the span of six weeks from our departure from the Boston Navy Yard, we had taken four suspected slavers as prize, the French vessels ***Jeune Eugenie, Eliza, La Daphne*** *and* ***Matilda.*** *Once captured I despatched prize crews to each of the vessels and freed the slaves aboard them."*

"Wow. Four slavers captured must have meant many freed slaves and a boat load - you should excuse the expression - of prize money to divvy up with your officers and men."

"Divvy up? If I assume correctly that you mean dividing the monetary spoils from the captured vessels only one of the four, the ***Jeune Eugenie*** *remained as prize, the other three were retaken from my prize crews by the Frenchmen remaining aboard the captured vessels. As for the freed slaves there were only two found. I still considered the actions a success as we were able to completely disrupt the trafficking routes for the entire season."*

"Commodore, when you refer to the 'season' am I to presume

that you mean a rainy season of sorts? That would make for difficult navigating in your two hundred ton schooner. We had the same difficulty on my gunboat in the Southeast Asia monsoon season."

"Precisely. I set a course for Boston, arriving at the Navy Yard toward the end of July. Our lone remaining prize, the ***Jeune Eugenie****, manned by my prize crew arrived in New York more than a month later."*

"In the meantime, the pecksniffian French consul was feigning indignation that I and my crew had 'outraged the Flag of the King' by interdicting the four frenchy slavers and carried his huffing and puffing to John Quincy Adams who was then our country's Secretary of State. Adams, in my opinion never a man of courage or foresightedness, was content to accept the foreigner's protest verbatim and promised to convene a court of inquiry, assuring the consul that my actions were completely my own and not the policy of the United States."

"Today we would say that they hung you out to dry."

"I can tell you that Adams' toadying to the French demand to relieve me of command of ***Alligator*** *got no further than the Navy Department. Adams' insistence that I be relieved fell on deaf ears, although I did suffer a written reprimand from Sectretary Thomson, who spelled out my future orders with great specificity."*

"Diplomats! Nothing more than a bunch of self aggrandizing, pettifogging blackguards if you ask me."

"Nothing much has changed in that department, Commodore.

You can take that to the bank. So I assume that you retained command of ***Alligator?***"

"Yes. But not without an ordeal in the courts. Adams' wish for a court of inquiry was granted that summer. I had developed a working acquaintance with Daniel Webster, then a vice president of the Colonization Society who agreed to act as my counsel. The inquiry eventually found its way to the Supreme Court where Mr. Webster's eloquent defense of my concept of 'higher principles' prevailed."

"Higher principles?"

"Yes, Grandson. Simply stated 'higher principles' refer to the moral indefensibility and barbarity of slave trafficking."

"In November of that same year I again set sail for Western African waters in command of **Alligator.** *It was but a matter of days before* **Alligator** *and her crew tasted battle. This time our adversary was a Portuguese privateer."*

"It's amazing to me how you managed to encounter those small ships in the open sea as you do. I mean you had no radar equipment then and really couldn't detect any ship beyond line of sight, certainly only four or five thousand yards at the most under ideal conditions."

"Radar? That word is unfamiliar to me, but you are correct in your estimation of the range at which the lookout in the crow's nest can detect another vessel. As for the probability of meeting other ships you must remember that most captains navigated their ships along established trade wind routes, making the chance of meeting

another ship less rare than one would imagine." May I continue with my narrative, sir?"

"Oh. Sure. Please continue."

*"***Alligator** *was following the wind on the morning of November 5th when we observed a vessel in the distance who was showing a closest point of approach at some 90 degrees crossing our bow and passing well ahead. An examination with my long glass determined that she was flying no flag. We continued our course which showed our bow on aspect to the as yet unidentified ship. As soon as she observed our approach, she shortened sail and ran up a distress flag, an international signal generally displayed by merchantmen in some sort of hardship. I gave orders to our purser to lay below and bring a barrel of pork and several caskets of water on deck to transfer to the supposed merchantman, believing them to be low on provisions. I then went below to my cabin to work up my current position of longitude."*

"Quite suddenly as I was laboring over my chart desk I heard what sounded like a cannon shot ripping through our mainsail! I returned to the deck to discover that our supposed merchantman was in fact a Portuguese twenty - two gun letter-of-marque, the ***Marianna Flora."***

"Arriving on deck the purser informed me of the true identification of the aggressor and remarked that shortly after I went below she struck her distress flag and ran up the Portuguese ensign. I gave orders that the pork and water caskets be sent below and had the ship's gunner break out shot on deck for the battle that had begun."

"The Portagee was raking our sails and rigging with shot from their

long gun. I gave the order for our brave lads to lie flat on deck to await the engagement that was about to unfold. If by God they declared themselves hostile upon raising their ensign then we would see to it that they would strike that same flag and surrender."

I could sense the excitement in the Commodore's voice as he related the details of the battle.

"We had approached the attacker to the point where we were finally within range for our six pounders to rake the deck of the scoundrel who had so foolishly tried to engage us and take us as prize. I maneuvered **Alligator** *into firing position and unleashed a withering broadside volley upon our larger adversary which decimated her upper deck. Those that were not killed or wounded abandoned their weapons straight away and hid below deck. I maneuvered again to fire a second broadside, then a third and a fourth. After twenty minutes* **Marianna Flora** *struck her flag and surrendered. She had suffered enough. The day was ours!"*

"Bravo, Commodore! The Portuguese captain did not stand a snowball's chance in Hell. If I may ask at this point, just what exactly is a 'Letter-of-Marque?"

"Your abuse of the English language astounds me. To answer your question a Letter-of-Marque is a letter issued by a sovereign government to a private vessel which authorizes said vessel to attack and capture foreign vessels that are considered 'enemy' and bring them to port as prize." In my opinion it is nothing more that a legalization of piracy by a nation."

"A license to steal, as it were."

"Ha. Yes, exactly. To continue, I summoned the captain of the

vanquished privateer and ordered him to explain his hostile action toward **Alligator.** *His ridiculous reply was to the effect that he was under the impression that we were pirates. I replied that if that were the case why did he shorten sail and display a distress flag? To that the coward could not reply. I then informed him that I was assigning a prize crew to take his vessel, crew and himself to Boston. Having done this I proceeded on my way to my ultimate goal of the Port of Freetown in Africa where I was to meet a representative of the Colonization Society."*

"At least this time there was no question as to your actions. I mean, after all you were attacked - an act of hostility."

"Not so, Grandson. Upon arriving at Boston the sniveling coward of a ship's captain brought charges which were, in due course after numerous appeals of verdict dismissed on the grounds that ***Marianna Flora*** *had acted in an extremely aggressive manner and such actions were an indignity to our national flag. The court did, however return the captured vessel to its owner."*

"Civilians!"

"What? Ah, yes. Well sir, **Alligator** *then continued on her course to Freetown where we were ordered to embark a Dr. Ayres of the Colonization Society and navigate along the African coast to locate a suitable area of coastline to establish our colony. While my orders read that my duties were confined only to navigate the coastline and examine the many harbors and inlets for such suitable colonization I soon determined that Dr. Ayres, while an agreeable fellow had not the fortitude to successfully discharge his mission under the adverse and potentially hostile conditions, which were soon to be the order of the day. I decided to assume command of this undertaking."*

"Why do I sense more of Nelson's 'creative disobedience' taking form?"

Ignoring my remark, the Commodore continued:

"After several weeks of survey we anchored at Cape Mesurado. I determined that this would be the best location for the new colony and expressed my opinion to Dr. Ayres who readily agreed. We began negotiations with the local Dey and Bassa native tribes, making little headway. A local tribal chieftain, King Peter who was chief of the territories that we wished to purchase was hostile to the idea, refusing to meet with us to discuss the proposed purchase. After numerous requests sent to the King via one of his tribal headmen a messenger from the King sent word that he would grant our request but only on the condition that the meeting take place in his village which was located some miles inland from the Cape."

"Hm. Sounds to me like you are being set up, you know, a trap."

"Robert, I **do** *wish that you would hold your interruptions to a minimum as they disrupt my narrative. Of course it was a trap. The King had other plans for us."*

"You didn't go, of course. Or did you?"

The Commodore heaved a rather loud sigh:

"Have you been listening to anything that I have said up to this point, sir? Of course we went to his village for the meeting. I had determined that this would be the only avenue available to us if we were to complete our orders successfully. I must say that it took

some persuasion to convince Dr. Ayres but he eventually agreed to accompany us to the King's village."

"To demonstrate that our objectives were peaceful I ordered that our traveling party be unarmed. Unbeknownst to our guide and the members of our expedition I had secreted a pair of small pistols in my coat pocket to use only in a dire emergency. Our guide took us through several days of thick jungle, mud and water. The heat was almost unbearable but I still wore my coat with the pistols in each pocket to fend off any attempt at treachery."

"Finally we arrived at the village where we observed the natives gathered naked around the 'palaver hall' as our guide referred to it, a large thatched building in the center of the village. The natives were buzzing with excitement. We were led into the hall and offered seats on mats spread out on the dirt floor. The main village headman announced the arrival of King Peter, a smallish older man with what seemed to be a perpetual scowl on his face."

"Giving the appropriate respect to the King, I enumerated our objectives in a pleasant and respectful manner, assuring the King that we had no interest in establishing an American Colony on African soil, as the British had done to the north. The King muttered some response in his native tongue which caused the natives in the palaver hall to shout excitedly and beat their weapons on their shields. He then responded directly to me, saying that our utterances were a deception, that I was not an emissary but rather a military personage intent on conquering the tribes and establishing the land for America. He continued in a louder tone that he knew that I had already captured many slave traders and had freed the slaves, thereby infringing upon his profitable business of human misery. He further stated that our party had no business in entering his village where no white man had been before and

that he considered this to be a particularly egregious affront. I at once knew that he must have been receiving information about our mission from someone outside the village. Looking about the natives in the hall I saw the presence of a mulatto standing close by the King. I knew then that he must be the informant, that we had been deceived and were in great peril. I glanced at Dr. Ayres who appeared to be saying a prayer to his maker under his breath."

"At that moment the King shouted something in his native tongue that caused even greater excitement to those assembled. The armed savages began to move toward our party in a hostile manner. I immediately sprang to my feet and brandished the pistols that I had secreted, giving one to Dr. Ayres and pointing the other directly at the King's head. The savages fell back. I instructed Dr. Ayres to shoot the mulatto if he or the assembled natives made any threatening move toward our party."

"Raising my free arm toward the heaven while pointing the pistol toward the King I again explained in a forceful and thundering voice the motives behind our mission and that our presence on the Cape would benefit rather than harm his subjects, and that if he did not honor the treaty as proposed on the morrow God almighty would wreak terrible vengeance upon the King and his peoples. Further I acknowledged that he had the option to choose war on this spot but that he would be the first casualty, that I was an excellent shot and the first bullet in the fracas would find itself between his royal eyes."

"When our translator relayed this to the King, the monarch was overcome with great fear and began to shake. Seeing this display the natives in the hall fell prostrate to the floor, moaning in fear. The King, in a halting voice, then instructed the headmen and assembled chiefs that the treaty would be honored, the land would be ceded to

the Colonization Society at the agreed upon price of three hundred dollars worth of goods, muskets, rum and umbrellas."

"With the signed treaty in hand, we returned to the coastline where I set sail for Charleston. Dr. Ayres remained behind to begin transporting colonists to their new home."

"An amazing adventure, Commodore. I assume that the strip of land gained that day is the country now known as Liberia."

"I believe sir that you are correct. And for now I must take leave of you."

CHAPTER THREE

It was the fifth day since I had been released from the hospital but I was not feeling any better. The hospital internist had warned me that it would be at least a month before I would begin to notice any improvement in my condition. He also advised me that I should begin to titrate back on the pain medications after one week or so in order to avert a different and much more serious problem, namely an addiction to prescription pain killers. His admonishment notwithstanding, I knew that there was no way that I could begin to cut back after only one week. Maybe in ten days I'd see how things were and then entertain the idea. In the meantime I decided to get over to my desktop and begin a rough outline of my visits with the Commodore lest the retelling of his adventures be lost in a haze of drug induced confusion. I knew that once the old boy had decided that we were finished I would have not much to rely on save some dry and dull history text somewhere that didn't begin to convey the excitement, the adrenaline of Granddad's many exploits.

And so, a few painful minutes on my keyboard at a time, I began to outline the basis for what would eventually be my historical novel retelling the many adventures and accomplishments of the Commodore.

I had fallen into a routine of having only the kitchen range light illuminated in the evening. As the sun began to set, heralding the chilly November night I settled into the damned recliner and pulled the comforter over me and began to fade in and out of consciousness. One last hit of the gin in the glass beside my chair on the tv table and I was ready for a few hours of rest.

"Tonight, sir I will recount to you my adventures - which were many - in our Country's second war for independence."

The Commodore had arrived, announcing himself in that thunderous tone of voice that he must have used to order men about when in battle.

"Jesus!"

I felt like I jumped at least a foot in the air.

"You startled me, Granddad. Can't you find a gentler way to let me know you're here?"

Apparently the Commodore was intent on continuing his story.

"Let us attend, then to the business at hand. Upon graduation from the Washington City Naval Academy I was commissioned Midshipman with orders to report to Commodore Rodgers' flagship, the ***USS President****. She was a sleek frigate of fifty-four guns, the equal of any foreign warship anywhere. Included in her armament were twenty-two 42 pounder carronades and one 18 pounder long gun. She was indeed a fast, trim and formidable fighting platform."*

"Indulge me, Commodore. I'm not certain about the difference between a carronade and a cannon. The only carronade that I know - or knew - of was the ***USS Carronade,*** a platform for launching rockets."

"A carronade, Robert, is a short barrel cast iron cannon used for close-in naval engagements. Volleys from a carronade at short range can be devastating to an opponent, killing or maiming all on deck and severely disabling the enemy's vessel."

"As I was saying upon commission as Midshipman I received orders to report aboard the frigate **President** *which was at the moment berthed in Newport, Rhode Island. I immediately left our family's estate in Princeton, arriving at Newport on February 14th, 1812."*

"In my time many of my peers have remarked on my apparent immodesty in describing my comportment while carrying out my responsibilities as a naval officer and..."

"I am shocked, shocked to learn of such heresy."

"Your sardonic tone is noted and summarily dismissed. Your generation of Stocktons seem to have developed a cheekiness toward their elders that I find to be both distasteful and disadvantageous to our task at hand. Hold your tongue, Grandson and employ the use of your ears. Presumably they afford a channel to your gray matter."

"Touché, Commodore. Please continue."

"Yes. Throughout the late winter and spring of that year I proved to be a quick study in my role as a young Midshipman and I must

discard all modesty to note that Commodore Rodgers was quite impressed with my rapid progress. In early June of that year it became evident that our long festering resentment with British high handedness on the open seas would eventually lead to war. The British were not affording us the respect due a sovereign nation, impressing our merchantmen crews to serve on British warships, impeding our country's expansion in the northwest, embargoing certain of our merchant cargos bound for France and delivering muskets to the Indian tribes who were massacring the citizens in our northwest settlements. These indignities, these insults to our national honor could no longer be tolerated. On June 18th of that year we formally declared war on old John Bull."

"Upon learning of our declaration **President** *put to sea in order to seek out and engage any enemy vessel that we happened upon. It was only three days hence, on June 21st that I experienced my first taste of battle."*

"June 21st, did you say? What a coincidence! That day happens to be my birthday. I wonder if there is some cosmic meaning to that?"

"Yes. Well, Grandson I sincerely doubt that that is the case. If I may be allowed to continue….."

"As I had earlier mentioned, Commodore Rodgers had seen my aptitude and application of duties both naval and nautical and bestowed a great honor upon me. Henceforth when the officers and men were beat to quarters before an imminent battle my quarters were to be as top mainsail officer with twenty men armed with muskets and two howitzers. We were to rain down upon the enemy a withering hail of lead while the gunners below wreaked havoc

with the enemy's vessel. This was a great honor and reflected the Commodore's faith in my ability."

"In our first engagement with the enemy I must tell you that I proved worthy of his trust."

"On that very day our squadron encountered the British frigate **Belvidera**, *a thirty-six gun Britisher who upon sighting our squadron turned tail and ran."*

"Our squadron consisted of the Commodore's flagship **President** *and the frigates* **Congress** *and* **United States**. *We immediately gave chase and as our ship was the fastest of the three we overtook the enemy and in short order they were within gun range of our 18 pounder bow chaser cannon. The Commodore himself aimed and fired the very first shot which tore through* **Belvidera's** *rudder and into her gun room killing nine crewmen. That shot was the first shot fired in anger in the war. We continued firing with the bow gun as we maneuvered to attain broadside firing position.* **Belvidera** *returned fire with her stern chaser, inflicting limited damage."*

"The first of our broadsides was fired on our ship's yaw and only inflicted minor damage on our adversary's rigging. Several more broadsides were exchanged between both vessels over a span of a few hours, wounding several men on both ships. My maintop lads continued to pour our musket fire on **Belvidera's** *exposed decks with great accuracy, taking care to avoid the exchange returned by a British sharpshooter whose function in the fray was to kill as many of my maintop men as possible."*

"It was at that moment that tragedy befell our brave lads on deck. Without warning a cannon one deck below the Commodore's position on deck exploded! Two of the officers forward were instantly

killed and fourteen of our men were wounded including our gallant Commodore who suffered a fractured leg."

"During the confusion of the moment ***Belvidera's*** *stern chaser continued firing, inflicting damage to our spars and rigging while we recovered from the unfortunate turn of events. As a result of this raking we were unable to maneuver into a favorable firing position to continue the engagement. The Commodore reluctantly gave the order to break off from the fight and retire."*

"You told me earlier that you yearned for the smell of gunpowder and salt air and it looks like you got your wish at an early age. Must have been quite an adrenaline rush."

"I am not familiar with your term but I can tell you that the naval engagement with ***HMS Belvidera*** *afforded me great excitement and adventure. I was not yet seventeen and I will say that I eagerly awaited our next encounter with the enemy. From my station on the maintop I would deliver a message to old Jolly Jack Tar that he would not soon forget."*

"We do have a few things in common, sir. I joined the Navy as a seaman apprentice at seventeen but it was eleven years before I would see any real action. When I joined we were engaged in what was known as a 'Cold War' with a then global superpower….."

"Yes. Yes. Perhaps at some later date we will have the opportunity to discuss your naval exploits but for now my time is limited. Please allow me to continue, Grandson."

"Seeing as the damage to spar and rigging was not severe, the Commodore determined that a short period in port to refit our

ship was not necessary. The repairs would be effected by the ship's carpenter and his mates, and we remained at sea for a period upward of three months. During this time we captured many British merchant ships and sailed over eight thousand nautical miles before putting into Boston for a short refit. We then left Boston and set sail to intercept the British West Indian Convoy Fleet, following their trail of refuse to within one day's sailing of the English Channel. This caused great fear and consternation among the Shetland and Orkney Islanders. They were fearful that we would land on shore and burn the towns and villages much as Captain Paul Jones had done in the first war with Britain. I can tell you that in retrospect I wish we had done exactly that, as some eighteen months later the British burned our Capitol of Washington."

"But I am getting ahead of myself."

I could 'see' that the old gent was really wound up tonight. I took a sip or two from the bottled water on the tray beside my seat and waited for the next installment.

"Upon sighting our vessel when we approached the Shetlands the British Navy despatched several frigates to intercept and destroy ***President*** *and in all candor I can tell you that this task could have been easily accomplished save for the fact that the British captains had little desire to engage our Commodore who by his very presence in these waters had sent the British press into a sheer panic. Failing to make contact with the West Indian convoy we set a course to return to Boston for a much needed refit period. During our return voyage we captured no fewer than seven of John Bull's merchantmen and recaptured one American merchant vessel."*

I thought I'd butter up the Commodore a bit:

"I understand why Rodgers was so pleased with your conduct as a Midshipman. You and he appear to be cut from the same mold. Do you think that he saw some of himself as a younger man in you?"

"I have no answer for that query, but I can tell you that both the Commodore and the men had respect for this young Midshipman Stockton who, though not yet seventeen had performed so coolly and I daresay gallantly under fire. The crew had given me a second title: 'Fighting Bob!' Think of it, these experienced and battle tested men bestowing upon me the sobriquet of 'Fighting Bob!' I was even more determined to demonstrate that this singular distinction be not wasted. I was determined to achieve even greater heights in battle!"

"Think of it, Grandson, 'Fighting Bob!' It was not long after that the Commodore advanced me to the position of Master's Mate."

"Sounds to me that the last thing that the Brits wanted was to square off against 'Fighting Bob'. It gives me great pride to know that some of your DNA - er blood - is spliced with mine. You make me proud to carry the name 'Robert Stockton.' "

"In my Twentieth Century Navy we had no Master's Mates. Can you enlighten me?"

"I do not understand this 'DNA' thing of which you speak, but the title of Master's Mate was one that was bestowed on exceptionally promising Midshipmen who were awaiting promotion to Lieutenant. It was a great honor that the Commodore bestowed upon me and I vowed not to disappoint this distinguished man."

"I see. Today's Navy calls them Lieutenants Junior Grade."

"Yes. Very well. Having finished our refit the Commodore's squadron left Boston in October of 1812 to continue bringing our fight to the British. Our flagship **President** *led the way followed by* **USS Congress, USS United States,** *and* **USS Argus.** *Several days after clearing the harbor,* **United States** *and* **Argus** *departed on independent patrol. It had been only a few days earlier that our squadron had sighted the newly built British frigate* **Nymph** *and the chase was on. Our maintop sail was unfurled and we gave chase for several hours but old Jack Tar wanted no taste of our lead shot in battle. The Britisher spread her sails and outran us."*

"Hardly an auspicious beginninng to our cruise but as Providence would have it we next happened upon a British packet ship, **Swallow,** *overtook her and captured her after only a feeble effort at defense on her part."*

"What type of ship would a 'packet ship' be?"

"A British packet ship was usually a lightly armed ship of anywhere from ten to sixteen guns that carried embassy mail packets and other documents between England and her colonies and outposts. They were from time to time also directed to carry bullion and currency. This was the situation in which **Swallow** *found herself when we captured her and discovered more than three hundred thousand pounds of currency in her store rooms."*

"Whoa! Three hundred large! What happened to all that cash?"

"Your pattern of speech, Robert, is foreign to my ears to put it gently. How <u>*do*</u> *Americans of your century communicate effectively?*

"The **Swallow** *along with her crew and cargo were captured and*

returned to Boston. The currency I daresay was utilized to prosecute the war against John Bull."

"Thank you, Commodore." His condescension was beginning to irritate me. "Language is a dynamic and ever changing system of human communication."

"Noted. I shall try to be less critical of your responses."

"To continue, we remained at sea harassing and capturing British merchantmen until year's end, and attempted to engage a British ship of the line, the seventy-four gun ***Plantagenet****, which turned tail and ran. I can only surmise that once our adversary had identified our vessels as that of Commodore Rodgers' squadron they decided that discretion was the better part of valor. We pursued* ***Plantagenet*** *for more than five hours but could not overtake her."*

"Several years later after the cessation of hostilities the captain of the ***Plantagenet*** *stated that his ship had been at sea for a very long period of time, that provisions were low and the men close to mutiny. I prefer to believe the American accounting of the confrontation."*

"The Britisher was correct in his choice to avoid. We were well armed, well trained and spoiling for a fight. Had he chosen to accept our challenge we certainly would have prevailed."

*"****President*** *continued on her cruise until the end of the year taking several merchantmen during that period before turning home for Boston, arriving on the very last day of December. The ship began an extensive refit and it was during this time that the British began their blockade of Boston Harbor and the Navy Yard."*

"I would expect that the blockade of Boston cramped your style, as we modern day vulgarians would say."

"In actual point of fact, Robert, the situation was quite the opposite. The coastline of our great country encompassed more than two thousand miles which meant that old John Bull simply did not have the ships to effectively blockade all of our maritime ports. Our gallant Commodore knew that the squadron would easily be able to run the blockade that the British had assigned to Boston Harbor. We would simply wait until our squadron ships were fit once again for harassing the enemy and run the blockade when the wind and tide were favorable."

"So the squadron eventually evaded the blockade ships?"

"It was early spring - April as I recall. We had high tide and when clear of the harbor the wind was agreeable. The Commodore gave the order for ***President*** *and* ***Congress*** *to deploy the longboats and silently pull our men-of-war to a location outside the harbor where the winds were deemed favorable to sail. Silently we slipped past the one Britisher that was close by, filled our sails and stood out to sea."*

"Bravo Zulu, Grandfather - I mean well done. Your escape meant more trouble for British convoys, I'll bet."

"In truth, this cruise began rather inauspiciously. In early May we fell upon the 16 gun sloop ***HMS Curlew*** *and offered battle.* ***Curlew,*** *being outgunned chose to evade and she outran us."*

"At this juncture the Commodore ordered ***Congress*** *to proceed independently and we parted company, sailing along the Gulf Stream in search of British merchantmen to seize. We continued*

along this northerly course throughout May and June without having seen any of the enemy's convoys. By the end of June we were running quite low on stores and put into Bergen, Norway to replenish our drinking water supply."

"Our fortunes soon took a turn for the better after exiting Norway as we captured two of the enemy's merchantmen. It was a most fortuitous turn of events as we were able to reprovision our stores at the expense of the British."

"Not long after this event two British men-of-war appeared on the horizon. After some scrutiny the Commodore determined them to be ships of the line and ordered that we retire. Well, sir the chase was on! We showed them our stern, setting all our sails to avoid the more heavily gunned vessels. Finally after three days chase we had outdistanced them and continued our quest to disrupt the enemy's supply line."

"Sailing within the Irish Channel for several more weeks we captured more merchantmen before setting a course for home. It was shortly after that we became party to a most unusual encounter. We captured the **HMS Highflyer** *without firing a shot!"*

"How in the world did you ever accomplish that?"

"With deception and a bit of luck, Robert. I can tell you, I never tire of recounting this tale. Ha!"

"Allright, Granddad. Let's hear it."

"Ha-ha-ha. The Commodore had captured a British warship off

Newfoundland earlier in the year and discovered a book containing the Royal Navy flag signals. When ***Highflyer*** *hove into view off Nantucket on the morning of September 23rd, I believe it was, the Commodore ran up signal flags that indicated that* ***President*** *was a British frigate and invited* ***Highflyer*** *to come alongside for reprovisioning. Once alongside the Captain of* ***Highflyer****, a Lieutenant Hutchinson came aboard and was promptly taken prisoner. In addition to the prize we discovered additional British signals and other important despatches. The Commodore outfitted* ***Highflyer*** *with a prize crew and set her sailing for Newport while Mr. Hutchinson, no longer a sloop of war Captain, remained on board* ***President.*** *Hahahaha!! I never tire of retelling that tale. The look on Mr. Hutchinson's face when he discovered the trickery will remain with me throughout my journey."*

CHAPTER FOUR

The barely perceptible sound of my cell phone ringtone had interrupted Granddad's recounting of the ***Highflyer*** incident and delivered me back to my immediate surroundings. I had left the damn thing on in the back room that I used as an office and was more than a little annoyed about being returned from wherever I was. The cell phone by this time had gone silent, probably leaving a message on the voicemail that I'd have to listen to eventually. Best to turn the thing off entirely, I reasoned. If I had to explain about the accident one more time to a well meaning friend or relative I'd throw the thing in the trash. I began to raise myself from the recliner when I realized that at some time during the night my body position had shifted and the full weight of my torso had been resting squarely on my broken ribs. The pain was so intense that I uttered a moan that could have awakened the dead - so to speak.

I managed to get up out of the recliner and shuffled to the cell phone and turned it off. The clock on the wall read 0230. I had two more hours before my next scheduled pain dose but I knew that I had to load up earlier. Maybe in an hour, I thought or even better maybe half an hour. In the meantime I'd go to the guest room and pull the pillows off the bed to wedge them on either side of the recliner armrests. That way I'd be less apt to turn over on my side while I was sleeping. I positioned the pillows, eased into the chair to wait the half hour I'd promised myself….and promptly fell asleep.

"I trust that you have attended to that irritating noise that had interrupted my recounting of the ***Highflyer*** *incident. If you are quite ready I should like to continue."*

"Yes, sir I have. I apologize for the delay but your call is important to me. Do continue."

Apparently the cosmic connection had not been broken entirely and the Commodore had merely been 'on hold.'

"Having recaptured and sent ***Highflyer,*** *which was originally an American vessel, to Newport we then set our sails for the Port of New York to deliver our prisoner. Shortly after our arrival the enemy's navy blockaded the port until the end of 1814.*

"Sir, if the blockades were that easily avoided why not escape as you had done in Boston earlier?"

"As fortune would have it the time of year was Spring of 1814. Napoleon had abdicated as Emperor of France and the entire weight of the British Navy and Army bore down upon us. The British blockade was not easily overcome, thus ***President*** *remained in port until the cessation of hostilities."*

"I can imagine how impatient you must have been to get back into action."

"Indeed. However, our Commodore had received orders from the Secretary of the Navy to proceed to Philadelphia to assume

command of the Delaware Flotilla. As I was now his aide I accompanied him to his new assignment."

"Our flagship was to be the **USS Guerriere** *which was formerly the* **HMS Guerriere. Guerriere** *had been destroyed earlier in the war by our* **USS Constitution** *and was in need of extensive repair. Such was the situation upon our arrival in Philadelphia when fate played her trump card. The Commodore and the sailors and marines of the Delaware Flotilla were ordered to proceed overland to Baltimore City. We would soon learn infantry fighting tactics and augment our militia forces there."*

"A large British fleet of twenty warships strong commanded by Admiral Cockburn had sailed into Chesapeake Bay with the battle tested army of General Ross aboard. Cockburn landed Ross' army on the Patuxent River. Ross then began a march toward our Capitol of Washington. Ross' army was first met by elements of the Maryland Militia led by Generals Winder and Stansbury near the Maryland town of Bladensburg resulting in a complete rout of the Marylanders, due in no small part to the incompetence of the aforementioned officers and the cowardice of their men, who were observed fleeing willy nilly through the streets of our Capitol. Ross then advanced unopposed into Washington and proceeded to burn all public buildings to the ground."

"I don't understand why the Brits chose Washington when Baltimore, with its harbor would have been a much more high value target."

"High value target, you say? That phrase sir, has a favorable ring to it. With your permission I shall add that phrase to my vocabulary when describing past battles."

"I digress. Earlier in the year American troops crossed into Canada and took the undefended town of Port Dover and set it afire. The Washington burning was largely seen as retaliation for that earlier foray. The larger issue at hand was the peril in which Alexandria and Baltimore found themselves."

"A British naval diversionary force under a Captain Gordon was despatched along the Potomac to capture Fort Warburton. This was accomplished with ease, as the cowardly Militia Captain Dyson, upon seeing the British squadron, spiked his cannons, blew up the fort and fled along with 500 Maryland militiamen. In my opinion Dyson should have been court martialed and summarily shot. He was merely dismissed from the service. Such were the troubles that our land militia forces encountered throughout much of the war when faced with battle hardened British troops who had recently fought in Wellington's armies. They simply turned and ran. A national disgrace, I tell you."

"When the Mayor of Alexandria observed the British squadron approach he met Captain Gordon under a white flag and simply handed the Britisher the soverign town of Alexandria. All goods and supplies stored in the dockside warehouses and twenty-two merchant ships - twenty-two! - were taken by the British without firing a shot."

"It seems to me that Baltimore was the more important target. Why divide forces and worry about Alexandria?"

"Well sir, once Gordon had captured what remained of Fort Warburton the path to Alexandria and its port was virtually unopposed. Gordon simply sailed in with his force and a wealth of provisions were at his fingertips. I should tell you that once

Alexandria had been taken the path to Georgetown lay before him."

"After the sacking of Washington the Secretary and other governmental offices had fled to Georgetown. Hearing the sound of cannon in the direction of Alexandria and not knowing what was occurring a volunteer was solicited to ride into the captured town to determine the intention of Gordon's force. Being an accomplished horseman I immediately stepped forward and volunteered to undertake the perilous mission."

"A horse was procured and I set off for Alexandria in the dead of night, some dozen or so miles distant. The passage was without incident and I soon arrived at the outskirts of the town."

"The town was quiet, the citizens having retired and the only activity was the work at the port where the British were in the process of preparing the seized merchantmen for the outward voyage. I tethered my horse and crept closer to the docks."

"Sailors and marines were busily engaged in looting the pierside warehouses and loading them onto the prized merchantmen. Gordon's squadron lay at anchor, awaiting favorable tides to get underway. An officer was urging the men to make haste as the orders had been received to rejoin Cockburn's fleet for the onset of the siege of Baltimore. Another officer approached the first with an order from Gordon to return to the flagship immediately as the recent rains which had doused the flames in Washington had made the river favorable for egress."

"Upon learning of this I stole back to my horse and rode off at full gallop back to Georgetown to report to Secretary of the Navy Jones and Commodore Rodgers that Gordon did not intend to menace

Georgetown but rather had orders to rejoin Cockburn's main force for the Baltimore attack."

"Our orders from the Secretary were clear: The Commodore was to harass Gordon's ships as they transited back to join Cockburn's fleet. We immediately set about construction of several fireships and boarding barges to not only delay our adversary but to defeat them. The fireships with their kindling and explosives would ignite the enemy combatants and our barges would provide platforms for our brave sailors and marines to board the British vessels and engage in hand to hand fighting. If all went well the day would be ours!"

"And so your fleet of fireships and barges engaged Gordon's squadron and defeated them?"

"We did not, sir. Owing to a change in wind direction our efforts succeeded only in delaying Gordon's run to join Cockburn. After a delay of several days the Gordon squadron of eight warships and the twenty-two seized merchantmen rejoined Cockburn's fleet. While we had not defeated Gordon his delay would prove fatal to Cockburn's mission to take Baltimore. Gordon's foray was financially successful but our delaying tactics forced Cockburn to delay his assault on Baltimore for nearly two weeks which allowed our reinforcements to arrive and assist in the defense of the city."

"I assume then that Secretary Jones issued new orders for your men?"

"Correct. Our orders were then to proceed with all haste with the sailors and marines from ***Guerriere*** *and the frigate* ***Java*** *to Baltimore where we were to report to Major General Samuel Smith, the overall commander of Baltimorean defenses. Once there*

we received military training in land warfare to assist in the repulse of the imminent British invasion."

"Sailors as ground pounders. I would have loved to see that."

"Commodore Rodgers knew that the British fleet's support was critical for the success of General Ross' army on land as it marched on Baltimore. It was therefore imperative to counter the fleet's entrance to the inner harbor and provide Fort McHenry's one thousand man garrison with protection by creating a barrier line from the sea. I was directed to proceed to the Baltimore inner harbor with a cadre of sailors and commandeer sufficient merchant ships for a sunken blockade between the Fort and Lazaretto Point, thereby blocking the harbor channel entrance. This was accomplished right under the noses of Cockburn and the British fleet. The merchant ships were towed to a point between Lazaretto Point and Fort McHenry and scuttled to form the barrier line, thus precluding entry to the harbor and protecting the Fort's flank."

"Having accomplished this I reported our success to Commodore Rodgers who then directed me to accompany a detachment of some well armed one hundred odd men from the Pennsylvania Regiment under the command of Major Randall to take up positions on the Lazaretto Point. This battalion was drawn from our entrenched bastion on Hampstead Hill where we waited in anticipation for Ross and his brigade. It was at this moment that the Gods of War smiled favorably upon us."

"It must have been a very broad smile, sir. You are vastly outnumbered and facing a seasoned brigade of well disciplined troops."

"I must remind you that our overall line of defense boasted more

than ten thousand men and one hundred cannon. It is true that the Commodore's redoubt consisted of little more than one thousand and that our postion would be the first that Ross' brigade would encounter, nevertheless we were entrenched and ready for the contest."

"Meanwhile, General Smith had ordered a force of three thousand men under Brigadier Stricker to engage Ross' army along the North Point Road and delay or defeat their progress toward our position at Hampstead. Rodgers ordered me to courier intelligence reports and orders between the Bastion and the Lazaretto through the enemy's lines. One of my first despatches to Major Randall from the Bastion was that - incredibly! - Ross had been shot and killed by a bullet from one of our advance party snipers, thus turning command of his army over to a Colonel Brooke, a man of considerable less skill and bravado than Ross."

"Let me see if I am getting all this. Ross is killed at North Point on the road to Baltimore, you are risking your life relaying orders through enemy lines and sailors are manning the Hampstead redoubt ready to face the British Army in a land battle, am I hearing you correctly?"

"Shuttling though the enemy lines between Hampstead and the Lazaretto was fraught with danger. There was no time for stealth and indecision. I raced through the outskirts of the enemy's advance units, drawing fire and returning fire when necessary. At one point I happened upon an enemy picket who, upon meeting me raised his musket and fired. The fellow missed his mark, just grazing my left hand and while he was reloading I fired my pistol, sending him to his heavenly reward."

"It was at this point that Cockburn's fleet began the bombardment

of Fort McHenry. The fort was commanded by a Major Armistead who along with his men bravely resisted a British naval bombardment of nearly two thousand shells over a period of more than a day's time. As the major had defensive fortifications constructed the shelling accomplished only minimal damage and the British fleet withdrew to just outside the fort's gun range, continuing the bombardment."

"The entrance to the harbor was blocked by our sunken vessels, the bombardment of Fort McHenry had done little to cause its surrender and Cockburn now knew that the success of Brooke's army was heavily dependent on gunnery support from his fleet. He had vastly underrated the size of our forces at Baltimore and had discredited the resolve of our defenders to thwart the British plans for the city and its harbor."

"In a last, desperate attempt to win the day Cockburn directed that a large force be sent ashore after dark and in foul weather to slip past Fort McHenry in hope of causing Smith to divert his force to meet this new threat and allowing Brooke to advance into the city. Armistead was not to be caught napping and his men directed a withering fire down upon the landing party causing many casualties. The diversionary feint failed and the men withdrew back to the ships in the fleet."

"Colonel Brooke, who had replaced Ross when the latter was killed then decided that without the support of Cockburn's fleet there was no chance of besting our brave lads and withdrew from the battlefield, re-embarking on Cockburn's vessels and withdrew. The British had been defeated and Baltimore had been saved."

"Bravo, sir, for a job well executed. Did Cockburn mount another attempt to take the city?"

"He did not, sir. The British regrouped and decided that they would next visit old Andy Jackson at New Orleans with much the same result. Baltimore marked the turning of the war on the ground at a most fortuitous time."

"What made that battle so 'fortuitous'?"

"When Napoleon abdicated his throne and the British redeployed their resources to our hemisphere there were actually some areas of the country that advocated making a separate peace with the British. This seditious behavior was particularly evident in the New England states. The victory in Baltimore gave our Federal Government the resolve to continue fighting."

"I'll tell you, sir that I don't think that much has changed in New England since your time. The voters there seem to relish their independent streak and often take it to the extreme. They like to disagree just for the sake of disagreeing, not to mention that they have an odd manner of speech."

"There was a gentleman named Key who, while being detained aboard a British ship offshore observed the bombardment of Fort McHenry and penned a most inspiring tune."

"Yes sir. That 'tune' was eventually named the ***Star Spangled Banner*** and is now our country's national anthem."

CHAPTER FIVE

As the daylight hours brought a lessening of my discomfort I was able to spend brief periods of time at the computer pecking out a rough outline of all that had occurred over the past several nights. The visits from the Commodore took place in the wee hours and as my discomfort was more intense during those hours I had decided to cut back on the pain meds during the day and increase the dose in both intensity and frequency during the nighttime. If the old boy was a no show well then at least I'd be able to get some rest and relief.

As evening approached of the - I was surprised to realize that I couldn't even be sure what day post accident it was - I settled in and was beginning to doze off when that familiar sensation of not being alone came over me.

"Good evening Granddad. I'm beginning to feel a bit better today. What is your pleasure this evening?"

"Good evening, Robert. Let us continue our journey."

No pleasantries or small talk tonight. On to the task at hand.

"Commodore Rodgers had been generous in his praise to the

Secretary of the Navy regarding my keen abilities and coolness under fire and in December of 1814 I was promoted to the rank of Lieutenant. I had only recently turned nineteen, the war with John Bull was ending favorably for our young country and I was eager for my next adventure."

"I can remember some American History from my school days. I believe that after the Brits were defeated at New Orleans they threw in the towel, as it were, and signed a peace treaty."

"In point of fact the battle at New Orleans was fought in January of 1815 after the Treaty of Ghent had been negotiated. Old Hickory bloodied the British nose severely in that fight and in the process all but signaled the end of the Federalists who were bleating like sheep in Congress that the war was a failure. That battle also silenced the seditious tongues of the New Englanders when they realized that we had prevailed."

"So now you are a fresh new lieutenant, the war has been won and you are seeking another assignment. What came next?"

"I received orders to report for duty as a junior lieutenant aboard the ***USS Guerriere****, now refit and ready for sea. The Squadron Commodore was a gentleman by the name of Decatur.*

"Decatur? Commodore Rodgers wasn't commanding?"

"When hostilities with the British ceased President Madison offered Commodore Rodgers the position of Secretary of the Navy which the Commodore respectfully declined. He then assumed the duties as president of the newly formed Board of Naval Commissioners, a board which assisted the Secretary in the administration of our growing fleet.

"What sort of man was Decatur?"

"A man of vigor and aggressive energy I can assure you. Just the fellow to lead our forces against the Mediterranean foe when we finally declared war against the Barbary Pirates."

"In my Navy we would say that the man was full of 'piss and vinegar.'"

"Ha! Yes, crude but accurate. To continue: Our country's time at peace was short lived as war was declared on Algiers and the other Barbary States of Tunis and Tripoli. The Dey of Algiers and his minions had been preying on American shipping interests in the Mediterranean since the turn of the century. Our President John Adams, through his State Department diplomats had negotiated a treaty with the Dey that promised safe passage for American trade vessels in return for payment of an annual monetary tribute. I can tell you with great certainty that our Navy keenly resented having to pay this blackmail to these pirates but as we were in the process of strengthening our Navy we could do little at the time but pay the brigands. When President Thomas Jefferson took office the paying of ransom to the Barbary Pirates was temporarily stopped with a show of American force but soon after the Moslem pirates were up to their old tricks."

"When the second war with Britain began in 1812 the Dey, recognizing that our Navy was engaged in the British conflict, unilaterally abrogated the treaty with our country and began to seize American ships in the Mediterranean, taking the American crews as slaves and hostages. He knew that we were 'in extremis' and that our naval resources were committed to the war with Britain."

"Well sir from your accounting of the 1812 war it would seem that our Navy had held their own against the British fleet and was probably a developing major player on the world stage. It seems to me that if Americans are being taken hostage we would have acted decisively."

"Indeed we did, Grandson. Congress declared war against these pirates on March 2nd of 1815. This war was to be the sole property of our Navy and embarked marines. We were outraged at the thought of our citizens being enslaved and were determined to teach these rabble a lesson they would not soon forget."

"Commodore Decatur set sail for the Mediterranean with a ten ship squadron composed of the frigates ***Guerriere, Macedonian*** *and* ***Constitution****, the sloop of war* ***Ontario****, the brigs* ***Epervier, Firefly, Flambeau*** *and* ***Spark*** *and the schooners* ***Spitfire*** *and* ***Torch.*** *Commodore Decatur had designated my ship, the* ***Guerriere*** *as the squadron flagship but I was soon to move to new duty aboard* ***Spitfire*** *which was in need of a first lieutenant. I was deemed fit for the position and thus became the right hand of the* ***Spitfire's*** *Captain, Alexander Dallas. I had previously served with the Captain in* ***President*** *when he was a lieutenant and I a midshipman. He was directing the bow chaser gun crew during our encounter with the* ***HMS Belvidera.*** *There was, in my estimation, no finer officer in our squadron."*

"Soon after transiting Gibralter ***Guerriere*** *signaled us to accompany her on a patrol to seek out any pirate vessels that may be in the vicinity. We did not have long to search before encountering the forty-four gun Algerine frigate* ***Mishouri****."*

"Guerriere *immediately began to maneuver to overtake the enemy vessel and our Captain being the consummate navigator that he* *was kept pace with her taking care not to come between the two vessels which were rapidly taking position to exchange broadsides. In point of fact our approach to* ***Mishouri*** *ran us extremely close under the pirate vessel's stern."*

"Upon observing the tactical situation I approached our Captain and requested that I be allowed to climb out to the very end of our bowsprit to observe the efficacy of ***Guerriere's*** *broadsides. This permission was granted and I moved out to the extreme bowsprit end armed only with a pistol."*

"I tell you, Grandson, we were so close to the stern of the pirate vessel that I could have easily leapt aboard. Indeed it took all my restraint not to do so. I was caught up in the battle and itching to deliver a fatal blow to the pirate Captain."

"No one is more surprised than I that you didn't do exactly that."

"I was there to observe the pattern and efficacy of ***Guerriere's*** *broadsides, which were wild and scattered. After the second broadside I crawled back from the bowsprit and reported this to Captain Dallas and recommended that seeing as we were in a favorable position that we employ our 32 pound long gun to rake the enemy's deck with round after round of fire. The Captain gave the order and we began a devastating raking fire which, after thirty minutes had silenced the enemy's guns.* ***Mishouri*** *struck her flag and seeing as she was engaged with us as an enemy was declared a prize."*

"Nice going, Granddad. Scratch one Algerian frigate."

"What? Oh, yes. That and much more. After the battle we learned

that we had seized the Admiral's flagship and killed the Admiral along with thirty of his officers and men. Commodore Decatur assigned a prize crew to take the defeated vessel into Cartagena and we continued our search."

"Sir, it seems to me that if the Algerian flagship and the Admiral were eliminated within thirty minutes that this war wasn't going to be much of a contest."

"It was merely two days later while we were sailing close inshore the Spanish coastline that we came upon an Algerine brig, the ***Estedio****. Upon sighting us she turned tail and ran for the shallows, hoping to avoid our deeper draft vessels. Eventually she tacked too close to the shoreline and ran aground. I am certain that the Algerine Captain thought to merely remain there until our squadron resumed our search for other enemy pirate vessels and lighten and re-float with the tide. He was in error."*

"The enemy ship was too close inshore for our larger ships to engage but our schooners were able to maneuver within range to engage the ***Estedio****. It was while our ship was firing that* ***Torch*** *fouled our gunline with her approach to engage the enemy. Seizing the moment I requested of Captain Dallas that I be allowed to put the longboats in the water and with a contingent of marines and sailors board the* ***Estedio*** *and after some hand to hand fighting capture her and take her as prize. Captain Dallas gave the order and we debarked* ***Spitfire****, rowing at a quick pace to reach our adversary"*

"In the thick of it again, eh Commodore? About to taste some hand to hand fighting with those fierce barbary Pirates?"

"Bah! The vaunted ferocity of these savages was greatly exaggerated.

Their supposed skill in hand to hand fighting was played upon by the newspapers but in point of fact these pirates were ready to surrender after only a token resistance. Fierce indeed!"

"As I was about to say, when the other ships in our squadron saw that our longboats were rowing toward the **Estedio** *they too put boats in the water in hope of arriving before us. I beseeched my men to put their backs into their oars and they responded in a truly admirable fashion. We were the first boats to arrive, boarding the immobile vessel swiftly only to find the deck covered with dead and dying enemy from our cannon fire. After a brief skirmish the Captain of the* **Estedio** *gave the order to strike her flag and she became our prize."*

"Having led the assault that captured the pirate ship must have been very satisfying to you. I'm sure that Commodore Decatur was keenly aware of your skill and daring."

"It was both a great victory for our Navy and a personal tragedy for me. Horatio, my younger brother by two years, your great-great-great uncle had followed in my footsteps and received a commission as midshipman, serving aboard **Guerriere***. It was during this contest that dear Horatio was mortally wounded, succumbing to his wounds many months later. While I am proud of his sacrifice for our country I am deeply saddened by his loss. As young Horatio so admired my exploits I feel a certain responsibility for it."*

"I'm sorry for your loss. It must have been upsetting."

"Yes. We will not dwell on the event."

"Following the taking of **Estedio** *Commodore Decatur sailed our squadron to Algiers where he met with the Dey to lay down terms*

of peace with the Algerine pirates. A full measure of recompense was demanded along with the complete return of all American and European slaves and hostages. A guarantee of safe transit of all American shipping in Mediterranean waters without the payment of tribute was demanded and given. In return the Commodore agreed to return all Algerine prisoners captured in battle along with the return of the **Mishouri** *and* **Estedio.***"*

"Having dealt with the Algerines we then set sail for Tunis and Tripoli where the Commodore demanded and received reparations for previous damages done to American shipping along with agreement for safe passage of our merchant shipping."

"The Barbary War was finished by November of the very year it began. We had not only roundly defeated the pirates but we had shown the British and European powers that our Navy had become a force to be reckoned with."

"I suppose that our young country was on the path to becoming a major player on the world stage."

"Quite true, sir. Upon the successful conclusion of the Barbary War Commodore Decatur was relieved by Commodore Bainbridge and returned to America. **Spitfire** *also returned, destined to be stricken from the rolls. I felt a keen sense of loss about this turn of events.* **Spitfire** *was a nimble fighting ship with a well trained crew and were I to choose we would have remained with the Mediterranean Squadron. The decision obviously was not mine and so at year's end we set sail westward for home."*

"In my twenty year Navy career I seldom was satisfied with 'stateside' duty. I preferred duty aboard ships that were destined for foreign lands. I'm beginning to believe that I got some of that from you."

"Ha. Ha-ha. That may well be the case Grandson. I had no sooner returned than I volunteered for an assignment with Commodore Chauncey's squadron which was soon to deploy for the Mediterranean and assume the duties as our country's Mediterranean Squadron. It was there that I would remain serving under several commodores for several years. It was there also when I would be given my first command and fight my first of several duels."

"Duels? My God! You hadn't had enough adventure in your assignments that you had to go fight duels? I can't believe what I'm hearing!"

"Let me assure you sir that not only were duels fought among opponents of equal social standing they were looked upon as a measure of acquiring respect among one's peers. I was from a family of landed lawyers and judges while many of my contemporaries were of seagoing or naval background. Duelling became for me a means to equal standing among these young officers."

"Sheesh! You shot your brother officers to achieve respect and social standing? Seems like a waste of manpower to me, moral objections notwithstanding."

"Duelling among equals was an accepted practice in the navies of the civilized world at the time. If a personal insult to a gentleman was uttered and an apology not forthcoming a duel was the method of the offended party to extract satisfaction. Additionally if an officer from a foreign navy were to insult the flag of our country or cast aspersions on her officers a duel was the method to settle the

affront. In point of fact I believe that I am correct in saying that more American naval officers were killed or wounded as a result of duelling than as a result of hostilities during the three wars of the first half our century. Our Commodore Decatur himself fought two duels in later years and was killed in the second duel by a Commodore Barron. Barron fancied himself slighted by our Commodore who had served in an earlier court martial in which this fellow Barron had been found guilty of unpreparedness."

"Breaking even in your duelling contests can spoil a guy's whole day."

"What? Oh. Yes, I believe I understand your remark. I myself fought three successful duels in my lifetime. My older brother Richard, who at the time was Attorney General of the State of Mississippi was less fortunate, having been killed some years hence in a duel with a fellow from New Orleans named Parson. A note found in my poor brother's pocket after he had been shot stated Richard's intention not to fire on his round. Would that Richard had shared my marksman's skill."

"I regret the loss of your brother and the pain that it must have caused our family at that time, but in the same breath I'm anxious to hear about the circumstances surrounding your duels."

"The first such incident occurred during my assignment aboard **USS Erie** *while we rode at anchor in the Bay of Naples. A Neopolitan waterman was provisioning our ship with goods from ashore. As I was reviewing the manifest in his waterman's book I noticed an earlier entry from a damned British officer which disparaged American naval officers in a most derogatory fashion. I was determined not to let this affornt stand as any officer from*

any foreign navy was free to read the same scurrilous entry in this vendor's manifest."

"As the offending scoundrel's ship was still anchored in the Bay I immediately sent a note to the officer demanding either an apology or satisfaction. The apology offer was declined and a duel was arranged to take place ashore at an agreed upon time and place."

"Both parties and their seconds arrived at the prescribed location and negotiations began with the dueller's seconds. The British had insisted upon a firing distance of much greater length than was customary. Apparently my opponent wished to have the honor of the duel without chance of being hit. These 'gentlemen' also insisted on a firing window of only the time that it takes for a handkerchief to flutter to the ground after being let go at chin's height. However ridiculous, I agreed to these terms and the prescribed firing distance was paced off."

"I admire your courage Granddad, what with fighting the Brit on his own terms but it seems to me that your acquiescence put you at a disadvantage."

"Not so, Robert. I had no reservation whatsoever after observing the Britisher's nervous demeanor. Coolness under fire and a steady hand carried the day. We exchanged fire on the first round which resulted in my opponent firing hurriedly and missing his mark. In the meantime I fired, striking him in the leg. He immediately dropped to the ground crying 'I am hit! I am hit! Are you now satisfied?' I raised my pistol and replied that I was not and to prepare for the next exchange."

"Your blood was up."

"You must remember that this fellow had not only insulted my honor but the honor of all American naval officers as well. I would only be satisfied after a second round of fire."

"And then on the next exhange you killed him"?

"No sir I did not. The Britisher would have none of it and refused to stand for a second exchange of fire. My opponent steadfastly refused my demand. Disgusted with the man's cowardice I left the field."

"One down and two to go."

"Do not think for one moment sir that I am given to duelling merely to advance my position and standing among my peers and seniors for that is not the case. In only one of my duels was an American officer my opponent. In that particular duel a young midshipman was heard making boastful remarks as to what he would do to me if it were not for my seniority in rank. I approached the young man and stated that I was unaware of any conduct that I may have directed his way that would cause him offense but that I certainly would not hide behind my rank if he wished satisfaction. I again told the fellow that I would be satisfied with an explanation of his remarks but to his credit he refused and a duel was arranged."

"I see. My remark was a bit hasty. What was the outcome of the duel with the young midshipman ?"

"The fellow fired first and missed. I would not fire upon an unarmed man and requested that he reload. My opponent refused, saying that he had taken his shot and would not reload until I had mine whereupon I pointed my pistol directly into the air and fired. After some back and forth among our seconds it was determined that all parties had received satisfaction and the duel was ended."

"That was a very chivalrous if somewhat dangerous path to take and I admire you for it. What became of that young midshipman?"

"Thank you. I cannot remember the fellow's name and his naval career has been lost to history. I can tell you that he and his peers were ever more attentive to their duties in preserving the ship's discipline. We had no further incidents which led to our first encounter."

"Well there is one more 'encounter' as you so casually put it that you haven't mentioned yet. I assume that your third duel was with a foreigner?"

"There was great animosity between the British and American officers when American ships visited Gibraltar. On one occasion the Captain of an American merchantman was arrested and thrown into a jail with the most scurrilous criminals and was insulted by the Guard Captain. The American Captain demanded satifaction from the guard officer only to be dismissed as a merchantman Captain inferior to the Guard Captain's standing. Our ship was in port at this time and I deemed it appropriate that this insulting behavior by the Guard Captain be addressed. As I was the only unmarried officer aboard **Erie** *and American honor had been sullied I undertook this challenge and demanded satisfaction from this so called 'gentleman.' My demand for satisfaction was accepted and guarantees were issued that I would not be arrested if I set foot on the Rock for the purpose of the duel. This guarantee of safe passage proved to be worthless as you will soon see."*

"They set a trap for you."

"So the scoundrels thought but they had not reckoned with the

tenacity of their opponent. An area at the very top of the Rock was designated for the duel with assurances that there would be no patrols in the vicinity. Upon arrival my adversary began to argue over the most basic accepted rules for duelling as well as insisting on an extended distance between parties and the 'drop handkerchief' window for discharging pistols. As the negotiations continued I became suspicious that a trap was being set to capture and send me to the gallows which the Governor of the Rock had promised to do should any American be caught ashore for the purpose of fighting a duel with a British officer."

"Well, Commodore with discretion being the better part of valor I assume that you hightailed it out of there as quickly as possible."

"Ha. Ha-ha. No sir. Once I realized that a trap had been set I immediately agreed to any duelling terms that the Captain desired. Faced with this he was forced to duel, fired and missed and was then seriously wounded when my shot found its mark. As I approached my adversary to determine the extent of his wound he confessed that a trap had been set and begged me to leave as quickly as possible. This I can assure you is exactly what I did, turning and running at top speed down the path toward the water's edge."

"Yes? Yes? Were you able to escape the trap they had set?"

"Commodore? Granddad? Did you escape?"

Silence. The Commodore had apparently signed off for the day.

"Damn! It was just getting good."

CHAPTER SIX

I spent all the next morning laboriously pecking out an outline of the Commodore's adventures in the Mediterranean as best I could recall them. After…what was it, three, four, five nights or more of his revelations?… I was eagerly awaiting each nightly installment. If no more visits were forthcoming our project - I was totally committed to finish this - would have to be scrapped. Here he was, about to be arrested and possibly hanged after having fought and wounded a British Officer at the very top of Gibraltar and……..and…..well, that's where the whole thing stood. The Commodore had left the building and in the process left me -you should excuse the expression - hanging.

Had he lost interest? Had a change of heart? Two nights passed uneventfully. No visit from Granddad. The next day I had a follow up medical visit scheduled and had all but given up hope of another visit from the Commodore. I was trying to figure out what I'd be doing with myself in those long, painful nighttime hours to pass the time until daylight.

The medical examination was uneventful, there really wasn't much to be done other than assess my level of pain and prescribe the painkillers that would help me rest in some modicum of comfort. This was done along with the obligatory lecture on prescription painkiller dependency. I returned home to load up on the next dose and sit in that damn recliner which I had come to detest. I would have given my first born to be able to sleep in an actual bed. Well, I thought, nothing can be done about it so load up, grab another gin and assume the position.

I was soon asleep.

Sometime after nightfall I awoke, realizing that I was extremely thirsty. I eased up out of the recliner and shuffled off to the kitchen to retrieve a bottled water. While I was in the kitchen that strange sensation came over me again, the sensation that someone else was in the house with me. I smiled and headed back to my seat.

"You have been conspicuous in your absence, Commodore. I've been waiting for the other shoe to drop."

"Pardon? Shoe? Drop? If you are referring to my recent sudden departure there were other affairs which required my attention. Do not bother yourself about them."

"Fine with me. I think that when we last met you were telling me that your opponent in the Gibraltar duel had confirmed that a trap had indeed been set and that you were set to hightail it out of there."

"Correct. When I learned of this treachery I began to run at full speed down a path between the rocks toward the harbor. I presently came upon a British lieutenant and a cadre of soldiers that had been sent to apprehend me. The officer was a rotund little fellow and had a sneer on his lips, sure that he had captured a Yankee

officer engaged in duelling. The officer and his men occupied a position on the pathway that led to the harbor next to a parapet-like structure. The pathway was completely blocked by the soldiers and the officer was laughing smugly at my having sprung the supposed trap that he had set. I knew that time was of the essence. I had to act quickly and in a manner that was completely uncontemplated by the chubby fellow."

"I sprang forward and seized the lieutenant, forcing his head in a grip under my arm...."

"A HEADLOCK! OW!"

I must remember not to make these sudden motions. That hurt!

"As I was about to say before your undisciplined outburst, I grabbed the fellow by the head and neck and leaped from the parapet, the two of us tumbling down the rocky slope toward the mountain bottom. The soldiers above were in disarray, shouting and gesturing as the porcine fellow and I rolled toward the bottom. I soon released the Britisher and rolled to the bottom, covered with dirt and blood. I had gathered many scrapes and bruises during my descent."

"Ha! Amazing! I'll bet that the Brits were fit to be tied."

"As I reached the bottom of the mountain I could hear the soldiers rushing down the path to intercept me. There was a considerable distance remaining to reach our longboat which was waiting at the pier. I was near exhaustion from the preceeding events and was unsure as to my ability to cover the remaining distance which led directly through the town. I was in peril of capture by the British."

"Then, As God himself is my witness, it was at this very moment that a gentleman appeared on horseback taking a leisurely evening canter. I accosted the fellow and asked permission to borrow his mount for the remaining distance to the boat. He most naturally declined and as I could hear the shouts and footsteps gaining on me I grabbed the fellow by the leg and pulled him from his mount, gained the saddle and departed at a full gallop through Gibraltar town for the longboat waiting for me at pierside. I arrived there, dismounted and rushed to the boat, ordering the men to row as if their lives depended on it, whereupon I collapsed in a full faint in the bow. When we arrived at **Erie** *I was lifted from the longboat and taken to my quarters where I was laid upon my bed remaining there for nearly a day."*

"Amazing! Absolutely amazing! And that was the last of your duels?"

"That is correct, sir. I was soon to assume command of the **Erie.** *There were other shipboard matters relevant to command which required my skills in both diplomacy and leadership. I was to assume command of my ship under quite delicate circumstances."*

"My guess is that you approached this new challenge as you had the others: With forthrightness and certainty of your actions."

There it was again. I was beginning to sound like the Commodore. A little polishing of my grammar couldn't be all bad, I thought to myself.

"The pattern of speech that you affect, sir is in need of more than mere polish. It is all that I can do to decipher your cryptic manner of speaking."

Note to self: He can hear you when you have thoughts.

"Sir, you have stated that your assuming command of ***Erie*** was not under normal circumstances. What was going on?"

"It was the summer of 1819. We were anchored in the Bay of Naples when a most unusual occurrence caused the formation of a Court Martial Board aboard our flagship **Guerriere**. *A Marine by the name of Sloane had viciously assaulted a sailor with intent to murder. Having been found guilty, Sloane was clapped in irons to await the reading of the verdict and sentencing. In the meantime members of the Board had gone ashore and reconvened in a hotel in Naples to finish writing the Board findings. When these findings were presented to Commodore Stewart who was now the Mediterranean Squadron Commander he declared that the proceedings and conclusion of the Board were null and void as the Board had reassembled on foreign soil, that there was no jurisdiction or authority for the Board to render a verdict and directed that Sloane be released and returned to duty."*

"How does all that have anything to do with your getting a command?"

"If you will rein in your impatience, sir I am about to tell you. When the members of the Board, which consisted of four Captains and several lesser officers, received Commodore Stewart's directive they responded with an official letter, which our Commodore took to be insubordinate in tone. After much back and forth between parties the Commodore relieved the four Captains, Macdonough of **Guerriere**, *Ballard of* **Erie**, *Nicholson of* **Spark** *and Gallagher of* **Franklin**."

"Well then I assume that each vessel's XO - I mean first

lieutenant - assumed command of their respective ships. But what happened to the Captains that were relieved?"

"A most delicate situation indeed. My Captain, Ballard was relieved and I was given both command of **Erie** *and orders to receive the four relieved Captains aboard to transport them back to the United States. I was determined to carry out those orders and do everything in my power as Captain to preserve the dignity of the four gentlemen in my charge. To this end, I even gave up my quarters to them and took all my meals save dinner with my officers. I took my dinner with the four former Captains."*

"Well, there's an old saying that 'too many cooks spoil the broth.' I have this picture of these four officers, all of whom are senior to you giving you advice and direction aboard what is now your ship. It seems like it would resemble a 'Chinese fire drill' as we would say in my Twentieth Century Navy."

"Chinese fire drill you say? Ha. Ha-ha. No, Grandson that was not the case. When the officers arrived aboard I firmly but respectfully informed them of my intention to command this ship as I determined and would brook no other behavior while in my office as Captain. To the credit of the four they agreed and acknowledged that I was now in command."

"And they were as good as their word on this?

"There were only two occasions where I was compelled to assert my authority. The first occurred during the passage home. I had given the order to run along the slave trading route skirting the African coast, thinking that we may encounter an American slave trader to capture as a prize. We had been sailing along the coast for several days when late in the afternoon my lookout reported a sail on the

horizon. I gave the order to alter course to intercept the vessel and began to close her."

"It was nightfall when we were within hailing distance of this mysterious vessel. Several attempts at hailing her afforded no reply. I began to suspect that this mysterious ship was a pirate. To add to the confusion the Captain of the stranger appeared to have given the order to prepare for battle as much activity could be heard about her decks. Several more attempts at hailing were in vain. I gave the order to load and prime our guns and have our boarding party stand at the ready with grappling hooks."

"As I ran underneath this mystery vessel's stern I could see that she was much larger than **Erie**. *This mattered not as I had given the order and if the stranger did not return our hail she was bound to suffer the worse for it."*

"It was at this very moment that the stranger returned our hail in perfectly good English, not by identifying herself but rather echoing our hail to them! 'What ship is ***that?'*** *came the stranger's reply."*

"As I was giving the order to uncover our guns Captain Ballard approached me. He informed me that having discussed the situation with the other three Captains they felt that it would be prudent for me to answer the stranger's hail, that it was a perfectly normal and understandable course of action."

"Ha. I'll bet **that** sat well with you."

"I informed Captain Ballard in a courteous but forceful manner that no ship on the high seas could challenge a ship of the United States without identifying herself and to passively reply would be an insult to our flag. I further informed him that if he and the other

three wished to participate in the impending engagement that they should arm themselves, otherwise they should lay below and stay there. Captain Ballard then retired below to inform the others of my course of action."

"Giving the order to uncover our lights so the stranger could see our boarding party at the ready. I personally hailed one last time and gave them an ultimatum that should there be no response that they should be prepared to be boarded."

It was at this juncture that the Commodore chose to pause in his narrative.

"Surely you're not going to stop here? What happened? Did you board the other ship? Damn! What happened, Granddad?"

I knew he was still in the house and I could almost see him smiling, enjoying my anticipation. He certainly knew how to capture an audience.

"At that moment the stranger identified himself as a Spanish frigate, a vessel I might add, with twice as many guns as ***Erie****."*

"So the Spaniard blinked!"

I had been unknowingly squeezing the arms of the recliner so tight that my muscles ached.

"He did. Before departing I sent Lieutenant McCawley over to the other ship to certify that she was indeed a Spanish frigate. I further directed that once he determined that the documents verified her origin he need not search for contraband but return aboard and we would depart."

"Amazing. Just amazing."

Ha! You appear to have enjoyed the retelling of this adventure immensely. Ha!"

The old boy had obviously taken great pleasure in my reaction to the incident.

"If you please, Granddad try to remember that I am on the mend here."

"Psh! I have seen men with severe wounds carry on as if they were whole. If you are in some discomfort please refrain from whining to me about it."

"Hm. Do I want any cheese with my whine?"

"Anyway, moving right along, you had spoken of two incidents. What was the second?"

"Upon arrival in Boston the Captains informed me of their desire to go ashore to their homes. I responded that as my orders were to ensure that these officers would make themselves available to report to the Secretary when and where the Navy directed that they were free to do so should they agree to those conditions. I further stated that all that I would require was their word as officers and gentlemen."

"Captain Macdonough who was the senior officer of the four responded that they would damn well go ashore when and wherever they damn well pleased."

I knew what was coming. I thought to myself, 'Wait for it, it's bound to happen.' The Commodore ignored my thought and continued his recollection.

"I stepped forward, confronting Captain Macdonough who, although senior found himself aboard my ship. I informed him in a polite but firm voice that as Captain I would decide the terms of their departure for shore and should they refuse I would take any steps necessary to keep them on board. After some puffery on his part he conferred with the other three. A heated conversation ensued but in the end the gentlemen accepted my terms and gave their word. They were then free to depart my ship."

"Now that you're back in the States and have command of a ship where did the Navy send you next?"

"It was late winter of 1819 and ***Erie*** *was showing her wear and tear after four long years of service on the Mediterranean station. I received orders to take her to New York where she was to be laid up for refit. This refit would extend her length and increase her tonnage and take several years in the process. Captain or not I was still a relatively junior lieutenant and after taking her to New York I was placed on furlough, given my back pay and went home to my father's estate in Princeton where I would remain for more than a year."*

"Unbelieveable! You were one of their most gallant officers. How could they not give you another command?"

The Commodore gave what sounded to me like a sigh.

"The fact remained, sir that at this stage of my life I was only a junior lieutenant and others who were senior to me were also on furlough and would be called before me."

"Well it would seem to me that those who you had served with: Rodgers, Decatur, Stewart knew what stuff you were made of and would have given you a first class recommendation. You did after all serve them with distinction."

"In point of fact Commodore Stewart wrote a letter to Secretary Thomson which heralded my achievements and my selection as Captain of ***Erie*** *and I myself traveled to Washington to seek a new command but it was more than a year later that I was given command of another ship. That ship, which we have already discussed, was the* ***USS Alligator.****"*

"I recall our conversation regarding the ***Alligator.*** Nelson, the King Peter affair, the ***Jeune Eugenie,*** being dragged into court by the French. Are we about to rehash all that?"

"No need, Robert. There is more to my command of ***Alligator*** *than that of which we have previously discussed."*

"Full speed ahead, sir. You have my undivided attention."

"1822 was a pivotal year in my life. It was in January of that year when orders arrived directing me to take ***Alligator*** *to the Navy Yard in Charleston. Once there we were to undergo preparation to join Commodore Biddle's West Indian Squadron which was providing safe passage from pirates and privateers preying upon shipping in Caribbean waters."*

"Another adventurous 'pirate war.'"

"To be precise war was never declared as there was no specific country responsible for the taking and plundering of ships. The pirates were, by and large a collection of murdering, undisciplined

rabble. Confounding our efforts to stem these rabble was the propensity of Spain's colony Cuba to provide safe haven for these common criminals. Numerous requests for 'hot pursuit' into Cuban waters and on the mainland were denied by the Governor General of Cuba, Don Nicholas. We were also constrained by another technicality."

"Which was...."

"Your impatience knows no bounds, sir. The pirates had been given Lettres of Marque by the Spanish colonies that were in revolt against Spain, namely Mexico, Venezuela and others. These Lettres meant that the scoundrels were privateers that operated as 'Navies' against the Spaniards."

"The pirates had no respect for flags of other nations. All vessels that could be overtaken were fair game to them. The most egregious offenders were the pirates that took haven in the Havana harbor itself. They would wait for a defenseless merchantman to become becalmed, row out to the ship and seize her, her crew and cargo and return with their spoils back to the Cuban mainland. In the event that we were able to take these pirates prisoner Commodore Biddle insisted that we were to follow our orders from the Secretary to the letter and turn these scum over to the Cuban authorities for prosecution."

"I gather that the Commodore was no fan of Lord Nelson."

"Fan? I do not know the meaning of that word as used in this conversation. Biddle was better suited to diplomacy in my opinion. He and I remained at odds with one another for the next twenty or more years. My perception of him was that of a martinet. He concerned himself principally with how the Secretary would

interpret his every action. He was a cautious man, a man that eschewed action unless it was thrust upon him. I had no use for him whatsoever."

"Commodore Tuna."

"Pardon? What do you mean by that?"

"Chicken of the Sea. In my Navy we used that term for a commander that we thought was timid, afraid of offending those officers that outranked him."

"While I do not understand the term your explanation of it fits the good Mister Biddle perfectly. While the Commodore was not averse to putting his own men to the lash he had no desire to offend those above him."

"My understanding of that time period is that flogging was commonplace in our Navy."

"That is true sir, however I was dead set against flogging. It was a holdover from the British Navy that I found both offensive and barbaric. I preferred to lead by positive example rather than fear, and in later years I led the fight that ultimately led to flogging's abolishment."

" Those of us that came after you are grateful to be sure. Getting back to the topic of the war how did you manage to accomplish your task of sweeping the pirates from the Caribbean waters?"

"I simply ignored Biddle's directives. In the course of the next several months ***Alligator*** *rescued the merchantman* ***Jane*** *from*

the Cuban pirates, sailing boldly into a cove and engaging in fierce hand to hand combat."

"I tell you sir, my blood was up that day. Pistol in my one hand and my saber in the other I led my brave lads onto **Jane***, recaptured her after some intense hand to hand fighting and intended to despatch her to Norfolk with a prize crew. During the course of the battle the pirate leader was killed by a shot from my pistol which found its mark. When the rest of the cowardly rabble saw their leader fall they leaped overboard and swam for the safety of the Cuban shore."*

"Our efforts at eliminating the pirates had allowed us to recapture three ships as prizes: **Jane, Fox** *and* **Senegal.** *My intentions were to transfer temporary command of* **Alligator** *to my First Lieutenant, Mr. Kean and then embark aboard* **Jane** *with a prize crew of twenty-three men, intending to sail the prizes into Norfolk with* **Alligator** *accompanying as escort."*

"Seems to me that these characters were more bloodthirsty than their Mediterranean counterparts. The Barbary pirates appeared to be little more than hostage takers and toll collectors."

"Hm. Well, on the whole I would agree - if I am to understand your remark. The Caribbean lot were murderers and thugs that routinely killed their captives, hung the ship's captain from the yardarm and stole the merchantman's cargo and valuables. They held allegiance to no nation and savaged all vessels equally. Commodore Biddle's reluctance to challenge these blackguards in their sanctuaries produced no results. This is why I decided to follow Lord Nelson's strategy yet again."

"I can see heavy seas ahead."

"Unfortunately that is true. As we were proceeding to Norfolk we intercepted three pirate vessels off Sugar Key. A battle ensued and when the smoke had cleared we had burned one pirate ship, released the plundered cargo from the second and pursued the third into a cove where the villians escaped ashore. I then led a shore party of seventy men from ***Alligator*** *and* ***Grampus*** *in pursuit through the thick palmetto brush, exchanging pistol and musket fire as we ran. Unfortunately as the brigands were in their familiar territory they soon evaded us and I gave the order to return to our respective ships. Once aboard we set sail for Norfolk, arriving the following week."*

"To a hero's welcome, I would imagine."

"Commodore Biddle was furious that I had disobeyed his standing orders. The Cuban Governor General demanded that I be returned to Cuba along with my prize crew and prizes so that a 'proper legal enquiry' could be conducted."

"Proper legal enquiry my eye. They were going to throw you and your men into prison."

"Indeed. While I am certain that Mr. Biddle would have enjoyed my discomfiture at the hands of the Spaniards the Navy Department would not allow it to happen. Biddle, still furious at my having 'creatively disobeyed' his orders, relieved me of command of ***Alligator*** *and handed the ship over to a Lieutenant Allen. Allen then proceeded to sail her back to the Caribbean where a short time later she ran aground off the Florida keys. Unable to refloat her, Allen gave the order to abandon ship and set* ***Alligator*** *afire. She*

sank shortly thereafter and I assume that she lies in her watery resting place in the Florida Keys to this day."

"A sad ending for a proud ship. So you are again without command and waiting for your next assignment?"

"Correct, Grandson. A period of waiting that lasted almost four and one-half years."

CHAPTER SEVEN

My first encounter with the Commodore had left me with the impression that he was merely using me as a vehicle to refocus the historians on his contributions to the building of our country, and perhaps he was. He seemed to me to be a cold, haughty unfeeling sort that had no regard for me and had little familial feelings for someone such as myself in spite of the fact that I was one of his many direct descendants. But as our encounters continued over time I began to notice a softening in the Commodore's approach to our nightly conversations and supposed that he had become more comfortable with our relationship. I actually began to *like* him. His ability to paint a picture with his words, his mock disapproval of my comments and above all his bold and decisive manner had won me over. I found myself anxiously awaiting the late night hours when his visits took place, and made certain that the telephone was unplugged and my cell phone was turned off so that we would not suffer any interruptions during our late night "conversations."

I was soon to discover the reason for his "softening."

It was the late afternooon of the eighth day. I was updating the Commodore's journal - his adventures had remained remarkably fresh in my mind despite the Fentanyl's neurological effects - when it occurred to me that the Commodore's last remarks alluded to a four year wait between commands. I was eager to know whether this was a result of Granddad's troubles with Commodore Biddle or whether it was just a case of the normal "downsizing" that usually follows a peacetime period.

As afternoon faded into evening and evening slowly progressed to night my anticipation increased almost to the point of anxiety. What did Granddad mean when he alluded to the long period of time between sea commands? Was he still actively engaged in some sort of naval duty ashore? Had he been cashiered? Was he wounded or injured as a result of a yet untold adventure? And why the hell hadn't he arrived yet? Perhaps there was some correlation to the exact measure of gin and pain meds that facilitated his visits. If that was the case then it was time to revisit the formula.

I hobbled over to the medicine cabinet and applied another patch to my shoulder and swallowed two Percocet tabs, then headed for the kitchen and the slowly emptying bottle of Bombay Sapphire. Got to ask my son to pick up another bottle on his next visit, I reminded myself. Now.. on to the recliner from Hell.

Hooo. There it was. When the Perc and patch kick in it is just like a complete unload. I can still feel pain but I just don't care. I began to nod off, going in and out of semi-conciousness. I looked at the cable box clock, quarter after ten. Going down for awhile. Far down. Way down.

Suddenly I was awake! A voice was inside my head shouting, *"Wake up! Wake up, Robert. You must wake up!"*

Instantly I was awake and aware that I had crossed some sort of barrier between pain relief and coma. I glanced at the cable clock. It read one-forty. The Commodore had given me a 'wake up call.' If it weren't for his persistence in bringing me back I'm not sure what would have happened.

What irony! If Granddad had decided to take the night off I might have joined him wherever he was.

I had no desire to check out just yet. Time to titrate the drug doses back some before they caused me to stop breathing.

"I'm awake sir, thanks to you. Just let me get a splash of water and I'll be fine. Thanks again Granddad. If you hadn't arrived when you did I don't know where I'd have wound up."

"I have the answer to that Robert. Let it suffice to say that I would prefer not to have you around on a full time basis just yet. At least not until your command of the English language significantly improves."

I couldn't help but wonder about the Commodore's motive for bringing me back from the edge. Was he only concerned about his memoir that I was to write? Was he concerned about me as one of his many direct descendants? His appetite for action? All I was certain of is that I owed him one.

Now down to business.

"Well, ahem, when we last spoke you mentioned a lapse in sea command of more than four years. Are we going to cover that? And if we are what were the reasons behind such a long layoff?"

"Layoof? What is this layoof of which you speak?"

"Layoff. A period of unintended respite from one's profession."

"Ah. Upon returning from the Caribbean I was given orders to assist a senior Lieutenant Piercey in surveying the southern harbors of Charleston, Savannah and Brunswick, a most tedious assignment that was to last for more than three years."

"Hardly a plum assignment for a man of action such as yourself."

"Indeed sir, but while this 'chart making' assignment was a study in tedium I can assure you that were it not for this turn of events you would not be here in this room conversing with me."

"Hmmm. My guess then would be that you met, fell in love with and married the woman that would turn out to be my great-great-great grandmother."

"Well done, sir. You are correct. While in Charleston Lieutenant Piercey and I were often invited to social affairs held by the leading citizens of the the town. One afternoon we were invited to attend a garden party at the home of a wealthy exporter and banker, a Mr. John Potter. While there I was afforded an introduction to Mr. Potter's only daughter Harriet. I was immediately taken with her charm, wit and beauty. I knew right then that I would make her my bride should she be so inclined."

"That would account for all the Potter names in our family tree today."

"Yes. Miss Harriet Maria Potter had captured my heart from the moment we met. Her family had arrived some years earlier from Ireland and prospered. Her father had in the past had business dealings with my father The Old Duke and he wholeheartedly approved of our union. After a short courtship we were married on March 4th in the year 1823. Our marriage eventually produced ten children. My son and namesake Robert died as a child of an unknown malady which caused his mother and I great anguish. You, sir are descended from the line of my third child John Potter Stockton, a successful diplomat, senator and lawyer."

"Quite a pedigree if I do say so myself."

"Indeed. I must say that all of my sons led distinguished lives and served their country honorably. My daughters all married well into successful and influential families. A gratifying turn of events for a father."

"Well I am especially grateful to John Potter Stockton, my great-great granddad who produced the only other career Navy man."

"Career Navy man? Oh, I see you are referring to yourself. Well I suppose that that is technically correct. But we must move on."

Hmm. More of his condescension.

"Yes, well I'll overlook that last remark. Now it's 1823, you are married and are busy in taking depth soundings and chart making for the Navy. How long did that continue?"

"The tedium of survey lasted until 1826 at which time I requested and was granted a furlough to return with my young family to my

father's home in Princeton, where I would be engaged in various business ventures, newspaper publishing and, after my brother Richard's death while fighting a duel and my father's death I assumed control of the Stockton interests in new Jersey."

"Well and good, but what about the Navy? Had you resigned your commission to become a businessman and landowner?"

"My longing for a command at sea had not diminished. I continued to request furlough extensions and was in fact promoted to master commandant during this time. The complexities of a businessman, land owner and Georgia plantation owner had made it extremely difficult to extricate myself from these family affairs."

"Master Commandant? Is that the next step up from Lieutenant?"

"No, sir. Commandant is the next step from Lieutenant."

"I see. Then your 'Commandant' is equivalent to my era's Lieutenant Commander and 'Master Commandant' would equate to Commander."

"Yes."

"Well then when are you going back to sea? Or am I going to suffer the ordeal of having to listen to your business affairs?"

The Commodore gave a loud sigh.

"My business and political dealings at the time would indeed tell an exciting tale but as our original agreement was to give an accounting of my contributions as a naval officer we will move forward to 1838 when as Master Commandant I accepted orders

to serve as executive officer in **USS Ohio**, *a seventy-four gun ship of the line which was preparing to set sail for the Mediterranean as the flagship of Commodore Hull."*

"Fit and ready for more adventures fighting pirates?"

"**Ohio's** *orders were principally to show the American flag and protect American interests in the Mediterranean basin. However we had scarcely passed through the Straits of Gibraltar and made our first port visit to Port Mahon on the island of Minorca when orders arrived from Secretary Paulding announcing my promotion to Captain retroactive to the year before and directing me to proceed to London for two months where I was to deliver certain important documents to our Ambassador to the Court of St. James and obtain knowledge in certain areas of gunnery and ship propulsion."*

"Well, let me be probably the last to congratulate you on your promotion, Captain! Not everyone is selected for that high rank."

"*The promotion came not without a fight and some political machinations. Our two Senators from New Jersey took note of the fact that several names of officers junior to me were submitted to President Van Buren but my name was omitted. Senators Southard and Wall sent word to Secretary Paulson and President Van Buren that they would block all appointments until my name was added to the list for approval. After some back and forth, Paulson and Van Buren relented and I was given my promotion retroactive to the previous year."*

"You can be sure that not much has changed politically in Washington in the years since you sailed the earth. In fact it has probably gotten exponentially worse. Anyway, It's good to have friends in high places."

"I'm curious about your orders to London. Sounds like you are going to use your engineering studies from Princeton to learn about steam."

"The Gentlemen representing New Jersey acted to correct a political maneuver that was unjust. I have no regret concerning their actions on my behalf. And I can tell you, Grandson that I did not soon put this affront behind me. Messers Paulson and Van Buren would not soon be forgotten."

"Let us put political skullduggery behind us for the moment and move forward. Navies of the civilized world were quite interested in a new propulsion system which harnessed steam to drive propellors thereby eliminating the dependence on wind and sail. My friend Matthew Perry, himself now a Captain had developed plans for a side wheel steamer that was being studied. My thoughts centered around a steam warship propelled by a single screw type propellor that was connected to a shaft located completely under water below the ship's centerline. This would eliminate the side wheel vulnerability to naval ordnance. If the side wheel were disabled the ship would remain dead in the water and become little more than a gunnery target. A shaft driven underwater propellor would eliminate the risk of damage to the ship's propulsion. Naval cannon simply cannot damage it through cannon shot."

"At the time the concept must have been thought of as brilliant - and I'll bet that it was. How did you conceive of it?"

"While in London I was introduced to a Swedish engineer named John Ericsson. In truth the design was Ericsson's. Seeing the

potential for this method of steam propulsion in both commercial and naval applications I commissioned a London shipbuilder to build a steam tugboat to be used to pull barges in my business venture as a principal in the Delaware and Rartian Canal."

"I'll wager that I can guess the christening name of this vessel"

"Ha-ha. Your impertinence, Grandson does carry a bit of wit about it. If your guess were to be the **SS Robert F. Stockton** *you would win that wager. She was a sleek little thirty ton schooner constructed of wrought iron and was driven by steam propulsion through Ericsson's centerline shaft-to-propellor design. She may have been the smallest vessel ever to transit the Atlantic."*

"Amazing. How did she perform during the crossing?"

"She had extreme trouble answering her helm. Very sluggish to respond to course change. After consultation with Ericsson we laid her up for a brief period and repositioned the rudder ***aft*** *of the propellor. We then recommissioned her as the* **SS New Jersey** *and placed her back in service."*

"Problem solved!"

"Yes indeed. She responded to her helm smartly, a superb steam vessel."

"Your orders also mentioned something about ordnance or gunnery, I think. What about that?"

"A French colonel by the name of Paixhans had developed a cannon that was designed to fire an explosive shell. After some difficulty in

determining how to propel the explosive shell without it exploding in the cannon a fuze timer was developed to attach to the shell that allowed it to ignite after reaching the target. With the proper naval gun these shells could be fired on a flat trajectory for several miles. This cannon and shell represented a significant advancement from the old lead shot ball that required close in firing and caused only localized damage to the target. An exploding shell fired at great distance could wreak great havoc upon the opposing vessel. This was truly a great advance in naval warfare!"

I could sense the excitement in Granddad's voice.

"The Secretary had authorized me to negotiate with a Liverpool foundry to produce and deliver to New York a twelve inch Paixhans type gun for trials in our American Navy. This was accomplished and I returned to our country only to find that the Democrat scalawag Van Buren and his toady Paulson were about to attempt their revenge on me for my just promotion."

"Dirty work afoot. I love it. Let's hear all about it."

"Upon my return from England I immediately began to draw up plans for a sleek and fast steam-sail warship that would encompass the latest concepts in engineering and gunnery, a fast ship sailing in harm's way if I may be allowed to borrow a phrase from the former naval advisor to the Russian Empress."

"I don't see any instance of revenge there, Granddad. Unless of course I'm jumping the gun again."

"If by that phrase you refer to your propensity to interrupt before I have finished my piece then you are correct. You are indeed 'jumping.'"

"Now then where was I? Ah yes, the toady Paulson. The man was hidebound in his complete resistance to advances in naval warfare. He often spoke of being 'steamed to death' and became effusive when speaking of the grace and beauty of the pure sailing vessel."

"Nevertheless I persisted in my submissions of plans and drawings for the modern naval steam vessels only to be rebuffed each time. The exchanges of correspondence regarding this matter became quite harsh over time."

"Well sir I can tell you that in my twenty year navy career I sailed in many a steam powered warship so I assume that you won the argument."

"Your assumption would be premature. In order to silence me Paulson reassigned me to inspect timber for use in our navy shipyards."

"I can't believe it! Timber inspector! How the hell did you ever escape that?"

"It was an insult to my honor and an attempt to force me from the active rolls of the Navy. The situation dictated action on a political front. I was determined to do everything within my power to drive these two scoundrels from their high office."

"Sounds to me like you have a real problem there. The Secretary of the Navy is your immediate boss and the President is the Commander-in Chief. You can hardly take any action against them without jeopardizing your - what is it at this point?- twenty-eight year Navy career."

"Ha! I have you there, Grandson. That would have been the case

had I remained on the active rolls at the time. Rather than suffer the ennui of gazing at cut timber I requested and was granted a two year furlough from active service and immediately embarked on a speaking tour throughout our great state on behalf of the Whig presidential ticket of William Henry Harrison and his running mate John Tyler."

"As we would say today, 'paybacks can be hell.'"

"I will admit to being driven by political revenge at first however as my efforts on their behalf progressed I became more and more convinced that Van Buren and the Democrats had succumbed to the influence of the Jacksonians which favored a dominant Executive Branch of government. I favored most strongly Jefferson's philosophy of the equal balance of power between Executive and Congress with the Supreme Court adjudicating constitutional issues. This principle, along with the soverign rights of states became my rallying point."

"Not having an American History textbook at my fingertips and being a bit addled what with all these painkillers at work I'll have to display my ignorance and ask what happened - although I do know that your Navy service was not yet finished."

"General Harrison won the election with a slim majority of popular vote and a landslide electoral vote. The effete, champagne sipping Van Buren was turned out of office. His lackey Paulson was also shown the door when the General took office."

"Our fair state of New Jersey voted overwhelmingly for the General and Senator Tyler. To demonstrate their appreciation for my efforts on their behalf I was offered the Position of Secretary of the Navy,

which I respectfully declined. I was even approached by the Whig party to run for the open Senate seat from New Jersey which I also declined."

"I would expect you would. You are a man of the sea. I just don't see you as saddled to a desk."

"Saddled to a desk. Ha. Another phrase that I may borrow from time to time. You are correct. It was time to extract a quid pro quo for my part in delivering our state to the General."

"The spoils of politics as it were. What 'Quid' was there to be for your 'Quo?'"

"Hahahaha! I must say, Grandson you do have moments of wit about you. Paulson's replacement was a fellow named Abel Upshur. Mr. Upshur had assured me that I would be allowed to build a 600 ton steamer equipped with the most modern of naval cannon."

"And I assume that this promise was guaranteed by President Harrison for whom you had so diligently campaigned?"

"In point of fact it was President ***Tyler*** *who made the guarantee. Within one month after taking office our President was dead as a result of a particularly virulent case of Lung Fever. Vice President Tyler assumed the office of President as dictated by our Constitution."*

"So you finally have been given the go ahead to build your steam warship?"

"Indeed. I was appointed superintendent of the construction of the ***USS Princeton*** *at the Philadelphia Navy Yard. I was given*

leeway to select the project engineers. I was so confident of the capabilities of this new vessel that I personally guaranteed my own wealth assets to cover any cost overruns in the construction process, should there be any."

"Well it seems to me that you are constructing an innovative and fast gun platform. While you have given me a layman's description of the ship what about the cannon that she would carry as armament?"

"I can assure you that the naval guns aboard ***Princeton*** *were every bit as innovative as the host ship. They were to be mounted on a swivel carriage so they could direct fire to either the larboard or starboard side, they were equipped with arithmetic range finding devices that allowed the gunnery captain to fire their 225 pound projectile on the correct trajectory toward the target. Each cannon also had a device that locked the correct sighting trajectory in place. The projectiles were so devastating that each shell could penetrate four inches of wrought iron. You may imagine the damage that a shell of this power could wreak upon a vessel constructed from oak."*

"Ha. So it's my own relative that I have to thank for my stint as a hot shellman on a naval gun mount early in my career."

The Commodore apparently chose to ignore my remark.

"My colleague, friend and rival Captain Perry had established a weapons testing station in Sandy Hook. It was there that my cannon, which I had named 'The Peacemaker,' was tested while ***Princeton*** *was being constructed. Eventually 'Peacemaker' was wedded to our revolving carriage and* ***Princeton*** *was ready to launch."*

"OK I'm lost as to the time line. What year was it when ***Princeton*** was launched?"

"It is now early in September of 1843. The launching ceremony was a gallant and festive affair. Bands were playing stirring marches, bunting decorated her gunwales and she was christened with a large flask of whiskey, a truly memorable affair. It was but two short months thereafter that we easily defeated the British steamer **Great Western** *in a race around New York."*

"Ha. My middle aged great-great-great grandfather is part of the first drag race. Hahaha."

"By your tone it is obvious that you hold me up to some sort of ridicule surrounding the circumstances of this very important contest. Although I do not completely understand your comment I will attribute it to both your woeful ignorance of important historical events and your lack of respect for your elders."

"You're right, Commodore. I do apologize. Please continue."

"The **Great Western** *was touted by old John Bull to be the fastest steamer in the world. Well, sir I can tell you that it may be one thing to make that assertion but quite another to demonstrate it. A challenge was issued for a contest between* **Princeton** *and* **Great Western** *to race from the New York Battery to the open sea. We would soon see who was the faster of the two."*

"The **Great Western** *hove into sight at Battery Point blowing steam and, to the astonishment of all assembled, under full sail. I elected to keep our sails furled and, giving old John Bull a full quarter mile advantage began to easily overtake and pass her to win the race. The thousands lined along the shore gave a mighty*

cheer to celebrate our victory. ***Great Western*** *could no longer lay claim to the fastest steamer in the world. That mantle now fell upon* ***Princeton.****"*

"Must have been quite exciting I'm sure. Would I be correct in assuming that Secretary of the Navy Upshur would lobby Congress to construct more ***Princeton*** class steamers?"

"The Secretary of State, my old friend Daniel Webster had resigned his cabinet position and Mr. Upshur was now Sectretary of State. A Mr. Gilmer was at that moment the Navy Secretary. It was time for ***Princeton*** *to sail to Washington City to demonstrate the remarkable qualities of her construction and to provide live firing demonstrations of our two swivel mounted cannon, Peacemaker and Oregon."*

"I seem to remember reading something about this Washington visit. Didn't something go wrong? Weren't some Congressmen injured?"

"The memories of what happened during our firing demonstrations haunt me to this very day. I would have gladly traded my life for those that perished in this altogether unforeseen misfortune."

The Commodore fell silent. I sensed that he was reliving what must have been a terrible moment in his life and was attempting to put together words to describe the events of what must have been a terrible disaster.

"It must be a difficult moment to relive but if you feel up to it I'd like to know what happened that day."

Another period of silence followed my request, this one longer than his previous silence. I felt that he was gathering his thoughts and keeping his emotions in check.

Finally, after what seemed to me to be an eternity he spoke:

"It was a Wednesday, February 28th of that year - 1844, a cold and blustery day along the Potomac. We had been demonstrating ***Princeton's*** *propulsion capabilities and conducting ordnance and gunnery live firing exercises, principally to demonstrate the new technology of the twelve inch cannon. I had entertained many dignitaries and legislators the previous day. All were in awe of this great 27,000 pound weapon, Peacemaker. The day was a great success. All on board marveled at the prowess of Peacemaker. Champagne toasts were offered and stirring speeches hailing the new dawn of American naval superiority filled the air. President Tyler himself was scheduled for a demonstration the following day with some 400 odd guests who had secured invitations for the cruise."*

Another long silence.

"We were underway from Alexandria that fateful Wednesday the 28th with our guest party. The morning proceeded without incident, our guests were both stunned and amazed at the ability of Peacemaker to fire a 225 pound projectile more than five miles. After several demonstrations the guest party dignitaries went below for lunch and pleasant conversation."

"It was at this point that President Tyler requested that I arrange for one last firing in the direction of Monticello as a tribute to past President Jefferson. I demurred, responding that I felt that our cannon may be stressed and preferred to err on the side of caution. The President, who at the time was courting Colonel Gardiner's

daughter Julia repeated his request. He was most anxious to impress his future bride who, along with her father had embarked for the demonstration."

"I could not refuse this second request from my benefactor. With our guests accompanying me topside I ordered the gunners to make ready Peacemaker for one final firing exhibition. The cannon was loaded with charge and projectile……………….."

Granddad was having great difficulty finishing his account of the accident.

"…………..the order to fire was given…………….and damn my eyes the thing exploded into a thousand shards of shrapnel. Secretary of State Upshur was killed instantly as were Secretary Gilmer, Colonel Gardiner, a Mr. Maxcy of Maryland, Captain Kennon of the Bureau of Naval Construction, the President's Valet Armistead and two of Peacemaker's gunners. Scores were wounded including myself. Our President narrowly escaped death, having gone below just moments before to confer with a Virginia delegate. I tell you Grandson I would gladly have traded my life for those who perished in this tragedy."

"And now I must take leave of you for awhile."

CHAPTER EIGHT

I was astonished by the emotion shown by the Commodore when he spoke of the *Peacemaker* tragedy. I had listened while he relived the wounding and death of those around him during battle and never once had he revealed the slightest feeling save the excitement - the adrenaline rush - experienced by those engaged in mortal combat with an enemy, but when he spoke of the explosion aboard ***Princeton*** that fateful day it was all that he could do to control his grief. Through all of our conversations he had rarely shown any sentiment save occasional impatience with my interruptions but on this occasion I could see that the old gentleman was deeply affected by the explosion aboard ***Princeton***. When the Commodore broke off our conversation the previous day I felt that it would be quite a while before I would hear from him again.

I spent the next day shuffling around the house, determined to skip the pain meds during daylight hours and greatly reduce the dose at night in order to get some rest. Most of the waking hours were spent pacing back and forth, entering my recollections of the Commodore's exploits onto a computer file and (God help me) watching Jerry Springer TV reruns. Springer is enough to take one's mind off the pain at hand and substitute an entirely different kind of agony in its place.

I had decided to avoid any prescription medication until after eight o'clock in the evening. Non-prescription concoctions were another story entirely. Once or twice during the day a Bombay Sapphire and tonic would find itself grasped firmly in my left hand. The folks that distill that stuff should have gone to medical school!

The cable TV clock indicated that the time was seven-thirty in the evening, the house was dark except for a dim kitchen range light and there was a chill in the air. I decided that seven-thirty was close enough for government work and went into the bathroom and placed a Fentanyl patch on my shoulder and headed to the notorious recliner from Hell to get some rest. Easing gently into the seat I wrapped the comforter around my legs and shut my eyes, waiting for the relief that would soon come.

Now for some sleep.

"I trust, sir that this evening finds you employing a more effective method to manage your sedatives, for we are off to Texas on an extremely sensitive and important undertaking."

Glancing at the cable box clock I was surprised to find that I had been asleep for more than four hours.

"Yes sir, I'm fine thanks but I am somewhat amazed to find you here tonight after last night's events had such an effect on your emotions."

He ignored my reply.

"In a surprising turn of events during the 1844 Presidential campaign, President Tyler was denied renomination by his Whig Party who chose instead the verbose and bombastic Henry Clay as their nominee. This was principally due to the Whig resistance regarding the annexation of Texas. Texas had declared independence from Mexico and fought a war for that independence. Tyler favored annexation. Clay and the Whigs did not."

"While Clay and the Whigs were reluctant to annex, fearing a war with Mexico, the Jacksonian Democrats favored annexation and were not dissuaded by the prospect of war with our southern neighbor. Their nominee, James K. Polk, carried the day. Mr. Polk elevated me to the rank of Commodore and entrusted me to get underway in ***Princeton*** *for Galveston to carry the papers for the Texas annexation which had recently been approved by Congress. Once there I was directed to relay the papers to the Texas Legislature for their endorsement and return to Washington. Accompanying my flagship were the sloop-of-war* ***Saratoga*** *and brig* ***Porpoise.****"*

"Once again it looks as if you have been delegated to a rather ordinary assignment, carrying documents to be signed by the Texas people."

"While that may seem to be the case on the surface, there was an unwritten mission to be accomplished that was given to me by Mr. Polk himself upon my advancement to Commodore."

"You must understand that at the time Texas, having won their war for independence from Mexico by defeating the butcher Santa Anna at San Jacinto, held the key to our desire to expand our country's borders westward. There was resistance to the annexation of Texas in our Congress, led by Missouri's Senator Benton who feared that annexation would lead to war with Mexico."

"And I assume that President Polk saw war with Mexico as unavoidable if we were to expand our territories westward?"

"That is correct in part. The European powers were also interested in the southwest territories. Mexico, concerned that annexation would lead to American expansion westward was actively fomenting opposition to the annexation among the native born Texans."

"But the Texans were for annexation, right?"

"As I was about to say........(he paused to indicate his disapproval of my interruption)*....Texans were divided on the issue with a majority for the annexation. The President of Texas at the time, Anson Jones, generally favored annexation but not at the cost of war with Mexico. While Jones vacillated over the issue I despatched my surgeon Dr. Wright to pay a visit to major General Sidney Sherman. Sherman was commandant of the Texas militia, a fighting force of three thousand Texans who were in favor of a war with our southern neighbor."*

"Dr. Wright's message was simple and to the point: We would supply powder, rifles and other supplies needed to sustain a field force and maintain staging areas in Pensacola and New Orleans. In return for this aid our objectives were to remain secret. If our Congress got wind of what was happening in Texas Senator Benton would certainly withdraw his support. To this proposal Sherman agreed but still wished for Jones to endorse the operation. Sherman and Dr. Wright then traveled to 'Washington on the Brazos' to win President Jones' approval while I and several of the Texas Militia officers traveled to the banks of the Nueches River to begin strategic planning for the coming conflict."

"Well, sir you are once again in your element, clandestine

planning and preparing for a yet to be declared war against Mexico. And you say that Polk knew of this all along?"

"The answer to that, sir went to the grave with me and I see no earthly reason to respond to you in either the affirmative or the negative."

"Well it will make for more exciting reading anyway if you keep it confidential. I'm sure that your narrative will reveal the results if not the true motive."

"Would that it were so, Grandson but pride and political skullduggery foiled our plan to push the Texas border to the Rio Grande. When President Jones learned that General Sherman and I were planning battle strategy along the Nueches he was outraged that such actions were taking place without his knowledge. He asked my emissary, Dr, Wright if President Polk was aware of this plan to provoke a Mexican war and receiving an affirmative answer then suggested that I as a representative of the United States wished Mr. Jones to "manufacture" a war for the benefit of the United States. Once again the reply came in the affirmative."

"The cat is out of the bag, so to speak. That can't be good for either the President or you."

"Indeed. When Jones learned of our aspirations vis a vis the Mexican Border and our war plans he stalled for time, stating that he would make no decision until the return of the British Consul from Mexico. Jones was banking on the Consul bringing a final peace document. The Texan also stated that he wished to bring the war plans to the Texas Legislature for their consideration, which was to take at the very least several days."

"Why do you think that Jones was in fear of a war with Mexico?"

"If General Sherman was for something Jones was against it. Jones had been a private in Sherman's Texas Militia during the war and I believe he harbored ill will toward Sherman. If Sherman wanted to push the border southward to the Rio Grande then by God Jones would do everything in his power to thwart Sherman's move. Politicians! Bah! I wouldn't give a fig for the lot of them."

"As fortune would dictate the British Consul returned to 'Washington on the Brazos' with the peace document. Jones then declared his independence from American interference and sent the treaty to the Legislature, stating that he never intended to 'manufacture a war for Polk, Buchanan and Stockton' and completed his remark with an aside as to where I could go for all he cared."

"The place he suggested for you to go was quite hot and loaded with brimstone, was it?"

I couldn't resist that one.

"Vulgarity has no place in this conversation, Robert. Mind your tongue."

"I apologize, sir. But I have to ask…just what was it that Jones said about you?"

Another long pause. The Commodore's silence was deafening.

"He remarked that now that I had failed in Texas that I'd soon be

sailing off to the Pacific to incite war there. The sheer effrontery of this pipsqueak of a man's remarks galls me to this day."

"Well, um, isn't that what you did, I mean sail off to California?"

"My orders were to return to Washington to deliver the signed annexation agreement between Texas and the United States, which is exactly what I did, sir."

"And now goodnight."

I got the feeling that The Commodore left the house a bit angry. Heaven help Anson Jones if he crosses Granddad's path in his ethereal travels tonight .

CHAPTER NINE

Watching *Jerry Springer Show* reruns is like watching a train wreck: You know you shouldn't be eyeballing the carnage and destruction but somehow you just can't look away. There I was sitting in front of the damn TV every afternoon rather than working on the Commodore's narrative observing the overweight, toothless, unkempt and ignorant emerge from the shallow end of the gene pool to collect their dubious fifteen minutes of fame by titillating (pun intended) the nationwide audience with tales of incest, infidelity, battery and God knows what other trouble-in-the-double-wide trailer trash adventures that they eagerly shared with those of us who were willing to hang around and watch. I suppose it is a "there but for the grace of God go I" rationalization for watching this buffoon and his loyal followers but after a few episodes I could take no more. It was time to get back to outlining the Commodore's adventures on my computer.

It had been three or four nights since the last visit and I was again wondering if Granddad had thought better of entrusting me to retell his history. I had the feeling that his rather abrupt finish to our last encounter was in part due to his anger when he recalled his forced return to Washington. Angry or not I was keen to hear his view of events.

Would the visits continue? I certainly hoped so. I forced myself to hold off on the pain palliatives until much later one evening, working at my computer to get the outline of Granddad's Texas adventure on the hard drive. I finished up the last of it around nine p.m., poured a stiff Bombay to wash down the two Percocets and gingerly let myself down into the recliner.

Six hours! To have slept that long was a new record. Since the accident I hadn't been able to nap for more than four hours at a clip before this. My right side was quite sore, probably from being in one position for so long. I decided to get up and get a bottled water from the refrigerator.

Then it hit me. He was here. Not only was he here but I had the sensation that he'd been here for quite awhile without his usual 'call to arms' style of waking me that apparently was great sport for him.

An act of kindness? Concern for a relative? I decided not to push the envelope by making a comment on his apparent consideration for my recovery.

"Hello, sir. I've been waiting for the other shoe to drop, as it were. What sort of reception did you receive upon your return to Washington?"

"Hm. Yes, well as I mentioned during our last visit I had sent a letter off to Secretary of the Navy Bancroft expressing my bewilderment at Mr. Jones' perfidy and my intention to return to Washington with the signed annexation documents which, of course was ostensibly the original purpose of my visit. As for Mr. Jones, I consider his actions in this to be no less than traitorous. If Mr. Jones finds that to be too strong a characterization then let him

embrace the cloak of a coward. I will no longer dignify his actions with further comment. But I digress."

"Having no further business I immediately got underway from Galveston and left the Gulf, arriving some ten days later at Annapolis. Upon arrival I directed Dr. Wright to travel to Washington with the annexation documents along with my report of the events that transpired in Texas. It was some days later that I received a letter of commendation from the Secretary who also invited me to visit the Capitol to fully debrief the President. This was arranged and a few weeks later I delivered my report in person to President Polk and his Cabinet."

"I'll bet that the President was livid that President Jones upset the apple cart and ran away from another engagement with Mexico."

"I have no rational explanation for the events that followed. Mr. Polk and the entire Cabinet were exceedingly displeased with my accounting of the situation, much to the delight of the Texas chargé d' affairs, a fellow by the name of Lee. It was shortly thereafter that I was forced to relinquish command of **Princeton**, *a vessel that I had been closely associated with from its inception and sent packing with instructions to 'await orders.' Hostilities with Mexico loom on the horizon yet I am ordered ashore. It was certainly one of the darkest times of my long and devoted service to my country."*

"I'm not sure that I follow you. You stated yesterday that the Texas-Mexico boundary was defined by the Nueches River and yet today the border between our two countries is the Rio Grande. While I am no geographer and certainly not a historian I do know that the time period coincides with our war with Mexico. How exactly did that happen?"

"My recollection of events which of course is aided by hindsight is that the border issue was a red herring. Polk's real focus was on acquiring California and New Mexico which was then Mexican territory. He felt that time was of the essence as Great Britain, who was embroiled in a dispute with our country over the Oregon Territories also coveted California. I was only marginally aware of his true objective and was focused on expanding the Texas border and provoking hostilities with Mexico."

"It was at this time that Polk despatched a diplomatic envoy, a Mr. Slidell to Mexico wih an offer to purchase California. When the Mexicans discovered that Slidell's true mission was California and not compensation for their loss of the Texas Territory they refused to see Slidell and sent him packing."

"Polk had also sent General Zachary Taylor and his army into the disputed Nueches-Rio Grande border area where he promptly manufactured an 'incident,' claiming that American blood had been spilled without provocation. When Polk received word of these events he declared that belligerent acts mandated a declaration of war and the hitherto reluctant Congress agreed. The war with Mexico was on."

"I'm having trouble seeing how Zachary Taylor's actions differed to any great degree from what you and General Sherman had planned."

"I have often thought that as well. Perhaps the one difference was that Texas was technically still a soverign state when our plans were being formed. Once my squadron had returned with the annexation documents and were ratified Mr. Anson Jones was no longer a factor in the overall scheme, retiring to his plantation at Washington on the Brazos."

"This is probably one of my questions that irritate you so much, but I would like to know what happened to Jones after Texas was annexed and became part of the United States?"

"Not at all, Grandson. Exactly nothing happened to Mr. Jones. When the annexation was finalized he had hoped to be swept to Washington as the first Senator from Texas but that honor went to Sam Houston. Jones eventually put a pistol to his head in a hotel room and took his own life. I told you that the man was a coward."

"How odd, I mean to commit suicide because he couldn't get his way and be sent to the U.S. Senate."

"Odd indeed, sir. On the other hand the man was noted for his unstable and devious qualities. He was nothing more than a quack physician, failed businessman and scheming politico. Texas was all the better for his abrupt departure."

"But let us move forward. More adventure lay before us."

"By all means, Commodore. Full speed ahead. I assume that we are sailing into harm's way once again."

"Not immediately, Grandson. There was a time when I felt that my usefulness to my country had finished, that she no longer wished to avail herself of my service."

I must deviate from retelling the Commodore's story briefly to share with all of you a rather strange sensation that came over me at this moment. While I could never physically 'see' the Commodore during his visits with me there was always an image of him, a visual sensation in my mind of him if you will as the dashing and fearless naval officer dressed in his finest Captain's uniform and ready for battle. Tonight however a different sensation visualized itself in my mind, that of an older man, slightly stooped and very tired. This was so alarming to me that I had to inquire as to Granddad's state of mind.

"Sir, I sense that you might be a bit troubled and...how to say... somewhat disheartened with the recent turn of events since your return from Galveston. I hope that this vision is only temporary."

"Thank you for your concern, Robert. As you can infer from my recent remarks Nelson's doctrine of 'creative disobedience' can indeed be a two edged sword. We had gambled with General Sherman in Texas and come off the worse for it."

"Do I believe that I had been made a scapegoat in the Texas mission? The answer to that question serves no useful function, but my orders to refit **USS Constellation** *to make her ready for the impending war with Mexico were countermanded and I was left to languish ashore to await orders while my peers were at sea preparing for war. It was most...what was the word that you used...ah yes, disheartening."*

"As if to throw salt in my wounds Secretary Bancroft then issued orders giving me command of the frigate **Congress** *which was currently at anchor in Norfolk. My orders were to take her to join the Pacific squadron."*

"Well there you have it. You're back in the saddle again commanding a ship of war heading for action in the California territories."

My sense of the stooped older man had not changed.

"The sealed orders further directed me to ferry twelve civilians including women and children to the Sandwich Islands and deposit them there in our settlement. **Congress** *was to be little more than a passenger ferry."*

"As war with Mexico was by this time almost certain to commence you can imagine my disappointment at this current circumstance. I wanted badly to be in command of a ship or squadron in the Gulf wreaking havoc upon the enemy. Instead I was relegated to passenger ferry captain bound for the Sandwich Islands."

"Sandwich Islands?"

"You would know them as the Hawaiian Islands."

"Ah. Pearl Harbor. I was there in 1958."

"Yes."

"Let me get this straight in my mind. You are in command of the frigate ***Congress***, you and the ship are in Norfolk and you have orders to take some passengers to Hawaii. I do know that the Panama Canal wasn't a reality at the time so I assume you had to sail around Cape Horn and enter the Pacific via the Drake Passage. That's a pretty nasty stretch of water to navigate. There are high seas and squalls year 'round and much heavier ships made of steel have gotten into trouble crossing the Passage. I was part of the crew of a ship which steamed west to east through there in 1971 and we were battened down tight as a drum. It must have been a very hairy… I mean dangerous transit."

"I fail to see what hair length has to do with the Drake Passage so I shall assume that this is more of your assault on the English Language".

Apparently the Commodore was feeling better.

"To address your concern regarding our transit we did have a difficult passage, however I was fortunate enough to have as my executive officer Sam Dupont. Young Sam was a midshipman who served under me aboard **Erie** *and had often told me that he wished to emulate my skills in seamanship, navigation and leadership. It was through my personal conversations with Commander Dupont that I began to raise myself from the malaise in which I had found myself after the Texas affair."*

A different sense of the Commodore's image was beginning to take shape in my mind. His voice was again becoming confident and authoritarian, his image in my mind was morphing back to the dashing naval officer, ready to meet any challenge.

"Several ports of call were necessary on a long voyage such as this in order to provision and effect any needed repairs. Our first stop was at the Port of Rio where a few of our men became drunk and caused a disturbance that warranted courts-martial. Sam wanted the offenders to be flogged whereas I was dead set against it. I had always been disgusted at this method of punishment which was nothing more than a holdover from the British Navy and had never permitted it in any of my ships in which I was in command. Commander Dupont on the other hand was adamant in his view that flogging was an absolute necessity. He was a strong advocate of this barbaric practice. Our debate over the issue lasted for several days. Sam felt that on voyages as long as ours that the men would

eventually be impossible to control without some sort of severe disciplinary measure and flogging was the most severe of the lot."

"Well? Who won the debate?"

"Debates aboard ship, Grandson, are always won by the ship's captain. I did however agree to a greatly reduced use of the lash as punishment and then only in the most extreme and severe infractions of our naval code."

"To continue, our next port of call was scheduled for Valparaiso, Chile. Our time spent there was unremarkable. We provisioned and I then set a course to the south for a stop at Callao, Peru where I expected to receive naval despatches which would update our information on the progression of the Mexican dispute. It was there that I had a confrontation with the civil authorities over the unjust imprisonment of an American merchant captain."

"Ha-ha. Go get 'em Granddad!"

I was thrilled to 'see' that he was his old self again.

"Ahem. Yes, well as Providence would have it I was aboard **Congress** *one afternoon in Callao when we received a visit from an American merchant vessel officer from a ship that also happened to be in port. He stated to the Officer of the Deck that his captain had been imprisoned by the local authorities who were refusing to release him."*

My sense of the Commodore was of a robust, uniformed officer ready for any eventuality. He had recovered his old swagger.

"When I was informed of this injustice I departed ship immediately

for the local prison to interview the merchant captain as to what exactly had occurred. The captain informed me that as his crew was rowing him ashore they were bumped by a boat from a Peruvian Navy vessel. A brief argument ensued and the two vessels went each their separate way. Sometime later after the captain had left the dock the argument between the two boat crews resumed and blows were exchanged. When the captain returned to restore order the local authorities seized him and threw him in prison."

"Overstepped their bounds, did they?"

"I immediately paid a visit to the civilian authorities and politely requested that the merchant captain be released to my custody. I must emphasize that this request was delivered by me in the most civil and polite manner imaginable."

"But they wouldn't hear of it?"

"Must I remind you again, Robert, to please hold your observations until I have reached the end of my recollection?"

"To continue, the Peruvians were to a man the most bloviating collection of self important gasbags that I had ever encountered, American politicians notwithstanding. They continued to exaggerate the most minute of points, strutting and preening like cocks at sunrise. Eventually there came a point in our meeting where they refused to release the man. I then informed these silly dandies that if the captain were not released I was prepared to take hostile action to secure the man's freedom."

"Well sir upon hearing my ultimatum the mayor pleaded for time to send an emissary to Lima to determine what the central government wished to do in this affair. I then pulled my watch from

my pocket and told the mayor that if my countryman were not released within fifteen minutes I would lay **Congress** *to a position where her deck cannons would lay waste to much of the town. After a quite brief conference guards were sent to the prison and the merchant captain was returned to me, whereupon we left for our respective ships and bid farewell to the lovely town of Callao."*

"Bravo, sir! Well done. Would that we had naval officers here in the twenty-first century with your backbone."

"Thank you, Grandson. I then directed Commander DuPont to lay a course for the Sandwich Islands. We reached Honolulu on June ninth, exactly one month to the day from our Callao departure. After disembarking our passengers we provisioned and departed for California, arriving in Monterey on July fifteenth. Our war with Mexico had been declared some three months earlier."

CHAPTER TEN

I assumed that there would be little or no delay in the Commodore's next appearance as war with Mexico had begun, supposedly to settle Mexico's hash over a manufactured 'incident' along the Texas border but in reality to acquire California and New Mexico as United States Territories. The Commodore had played a significant role in this theater of the war and I was eager to hear the accounting of his exploits.

It was the evening following Granddad's last visit. I had followed my usual daily routine: Curse the idiot who ran the red light, remark on his questionable ancestry, work at the computer getting the Commodore's most recent recollections in a file, have a sandwich and a piece of fruit, watch a little TV and then prepare for the next visit from Commodore Robert Field Stockton, U.S. Navy (departed). Hardly what one would call sensory overload.

Time to stop feeling sorry for myself and get ready for the visit from beyond. Gin, percocet, some other little blue pill that had been prescribed and a 'floating' nap. If the Commodore were going to appear it would be within a couple of hours.

I didn't have to wait that long.

"Good evening, Robert. Are we ready for the next installment? It promises to be quite an adventure.

"Indeed I am, sir. I have you now in Monterey and war with Mexico had been declared several months earlier. As California encompasses quite a bit of land mass I expect that the Army played a significant role in the war."

"All of which we shall cover in good time, Grandson. Patience is a virtue."

I couldn't help but laugh to myself at an admonishment from a man whose trademark was that of impulsive action.

Goddammit! I forgot that he can 'hear' my thoughts.

"Let me first say that my 'impulsive actions' as you describe them occurred in the face of peril where there was no time to wait for approval from those in higher authority who were often hundreds if not thousands of miles distant. The circumstances at the time dictated action. I have always embraced Nelson's philosophy no matter what the outcome, and would do so today if I were whole."

"I must also say that your vulgar appeal to the Deity is unbecoming of a Stockton. If you must be profane kindly do so when I am unable to hear you."

"Noted, with my apologies, sir. If you will continue, I will listen."

"Very well. Arriving in Monterey on July I reported to Commodore Sloat who was in command of our Pacific Squadron. The squadron

was comprised of Sloat's flagship ***Savannah****, the sloops-of-war* ***Cyane, Portsmouth, Warren*** *and one stores ship. Sloat was pleased that* ***Congress*** *added another frigate to the squadron as the tension between his forces and the Californio forces was extremely high, Sloat having recently captured Monterey under the impression that he was authorized to do so which I might add he was not."*

"Sir, if you will permit a question or two for clarification purposes it will assist me in the transcribing of events in our journal."

"Very well, Robert. What do you wish to know?"

"First, I am not familiar with the term 'Californio'. Next, what gave Commodore Sloat the idea that he was authorized to seize Monterey?"

"Some years earlier the Mexican and Mestizo settlers that had migrated to California decided to secede from Mexico but had not formally declared their independence from Mexico City. These settlers, many of whom were retired Mexican Army officers formed a government and elected a man by the name of Pio Pico governor and seated a Legislature near Los Angeles. These settlers, then were known as 'Californios.' As the Californio Legislature had not formally declared independence from Mexico I considered them allies of our Mexican enemy. I shall elaborate further shortly."

"Where to begin? The Californios were divided into two camps. The southern faction, led by governor Pico controlled the area just north of Los Angeles southward to San Diego. The northern faction was under the control of a brutal and devious army officer, General Castro. Castro had been beset by a group of settlers desiring an American intervention in California. These settlers

became known as 'Bear Flag' rebels. Commodore Sloat had no desire to assert American influence in California and assumed a conciliatory posture that accomplished exactly nothing."

"It was at this precise moment in time that the British eighty gun warship **HMS Collingwood** *dropped anchor off Monterey. It had been established previously that Britain coveted California and was prepared to act had they not seen our American flag flying over the town. This must have disappointed them no end as they had planned to establish a foothold there and eventually transport some ten thousand Irish settlers north to the San Francisco Bay area, where we had begun to settle earlier. It was apparent to me that action needed to be taken quickly on both the political and military front."*

"Wait. Didn't you say earlier that Commodore Sloat had already moved to take Monterey?"

"Ha. Sloat had given an audience to a Captain Fremont who had been mapping territory to the north. Fremont was quite well connected in Washington being the son-in-law of Senator Benton and had a private audience with the President before leaving for his mapping expedition. While leading his men to Monterey Fremont had encountered the American 'Bear Flag' force and joined with them in their campaign against General Castro's Mexican army.

"Sloat had run up our flag over Monterey assuming that Fremont's meeting with the President had resulted in Polk's wish to initiate hostilities with the Californios. He felt that Fremont's support of the Bear Flag rebels was a demonstration of that policy. These assumptions by Sloat who was normally a cautious man led to his moving on Monterey and hoisting the American flag over the city.

Upon learning that Fremont had acted on his own, Sloat could scarcely wait for an excuse to depart the theater."

"I'm curious. How did Sloat extricate himself from the developing situation."

"In a meeting with me Sloat declared himself to be in poor health and announced his intention to depart for home. I suggested to him that he turn over command of the Pacific Squadron to me and allow me to carry out our country's objectives to conclusion. Sloat, while anxious to leave for home, began to have second thoughts."

"I'm sure that he was aware of your reputation as a man of action. How did you persuade him to bite the bullet and leave?"

"I simply informed the old gentleman that eighty guns or no our squadron was well equipped to defeat **HMS Collingwood** *should her admiral have aspirations to flaunt Mr. Monroe's doctrine. I further stated that we would be within our rights seeing as Sloat had already raised our flag over Monterey and declared California as a territory of the United States. I further stated that Captain Fremont and I had no doubt that we had sufficient military and naval assets to defeat the Californios who were divided into two opposing camps, northern under Castro and southern led by Pio Pico."*

"And so we bid a fond farewell to Commodore Sloat who couldn't quite bring himself to cross the Rubicon."

"Ha. Ha-ha. Quite good, sir. Sloat was only too happy to strike his flag and transfer command of the Pacific Squadron to me.

Within days he had boarded the ***USS Levant*** *and hightailed it for home."*

"Well, you are now in command of American forces in California. What are your orders?"

"My orders, sir are more than eight months past. Washington could not possibly know the situation as it existed. My actions that followed were based on the assumption that American lives were in danger in California and that our land and sea forces would take action to prevent any bloodshed."

"My first measure was of a political nature, declaring myself as officially the Commander-in-Chief of American forces present in California and Governor General of the Territory. I next issued a proclamation to the Californios that it was the intent of the United States to intervene and halt the barbaric actions of General Castro, a brutal and ruthless dictator. I stated that those who either wished to join our effort or render it no harm would be welcome, but those who resisted our efforts would be seen as the common enemy."

"You see, Robert, it was apparent to me from the moment of my arrival in Monterey that Sloat's appeasement policies were a failure. If California and New Mexico were to become United States Territories Castro and his army must be defeated. The flag of the United States must fly over the territory unchallenged."

"Well sir I would seem to me that you are going to need an army and someone to lead it. Who will asume that role?"

"After a few meetings with Captain Fremont it became apparent to me that he and I shared similar views. As Commander-in-Chief I

immediately promoted him to Lieutenant Colonel and enlisted his men and the Bear Flag volunteers into our army."

"I see, or at least I think I see. Are you saying that you simply attacked the Californios without warning?"

"No sir I most certainly did not. An unprovoked attack could not have been sustained politically. I began to initiate a series of correspondences with Castro and Pico that outlined the current situation. As Pico and Castro had not yet severed their Californio territories with Mexico City I reasserted my authority as Territorial Governor and Commander-in-Chief and offered them protection under the American flag if they would declare independence and initiate their desire to be annexed under our government. I further stated in a later correspondence that should they refuse I would be forced to consider them as allies of our enemy Mexico with whom we were currently at war and initiate hostilities to defeat them in battle."

"Well the fiscal and political mess that we call California today is one of the states of our union so my assusmption is that your 'invitation' was declined."

"In the most definitive of terms. To define the refusal correspondence as arrogant, boastful and impolite would be an understatement to say the very least."

"The die was cast. If you will recall I had learned much about organizing my sailors and Marines into a ground fighting force from my mentor Commodore Rodgers during the 1812 war. I now began to organize and instruct a naval ground brigade of some three hundred fifty men to prepare for what I had planned as both a naval and ground offensive against Castro's Californios."

"Where will you strike first?"

"I was reluctant to begin without first securing artillery support. I was fortunate in that respect as Sloat's premature taking of Monterey provided me with a number of cannon that were a part of General Castro's force that he had left behind. I merely put our ship's carpenters to work crafting wheeled carriages so that they were mobile. When finished I embarked our brigade and cannonry and set sail southward for San Pedro."

"I know the area well. My first Navy ship was home ported in...."

"Yes, Robert, as I had said earlier please allow me to continue. We may be able to discuss your Naval service at a later date. Perhaps you can write a journal about your adventures - after you are done with mine."

"Aye aye, Commodore."

"Thank you, Grandson. I mean no insult to you however my time with you is limited and I must press on."

Limited! Does this mean that whatever 'cosmic' channel that had opened between us was nearing closure? I decided not to ask as this would more than likely only further irritate him.

"To continue. Enroute to San Pedro I briefly stopped at Santa Barbara and left a small garrison force and continued on to our destination. Once ashore in San Pedro I despatched Colonel Fremont with a force of eighty Bear Flag volunteers and mestizo scouts southward toward San Diego as a flanking force and with

the remainder of my ground force moved inland toward Ciudad Los Angeles and Castro's main force at Mesa."

"While encamped outside Mesa I began exercising the men in simple ground maneuvers designed to confuse our enemy as to the actual numbers in our force. My advance scouts had detected the presence of Castro's spies who were gathering information as to our strength and fighting capability. As we had a limited number of cannonry I ordered that our few six pounders and one thirty two pounder be covered and disguised to look as if our artillery arsenal was much larger. Only the mouth of the thirty two pounder was exposed. As for the men I ordered that they form a marching formation four abreast with greatly extended interval between squads and drill in a large circular formation path, part of which was concealed from view. This appeared to the enemy spies that our force was more than twice the actual size."

"Once again you are proving to be a master of deception. Did your ruse work?"

"Shortly after our arrival emissaries from General Castro approached under a flag of truce. I directed that they be brought to me by the exposed mouth of the thirty two pounder."

"The Californio party had never seen a cannon so large and that was exactly the reason for my meeting them there. In a somewhat wavering voice their leader repeated a message from Castro suggesting that I accept a truce between the two forces until there was further clarification from Washington and Mexico City, which I declined in the sternest of tones. Time was not on our side as the longer the truce held the greater was the chance of Castro's discovering that our force was vastly inferior to his in both numbers and artillery."

"And you sent them packing?"

"Precisely so. I dismissed them with one to their own vulgarities: 'Vamoose,' I said in a threatening fashion and off they scurried."

"Shades of the ***Highflyer*** incident. Was the bluff effective?"

"After one or two more visits from Castro's emissaries he sent final word that if my men were foolish enough to enter the village that it would be the graveyard for my entire force. I sent them packing with a message for the pompous ass: 'Toll the funeral bells then for we shall enter at eight o'clock the following day.'"

"So you prepared to do battle with a force vastly superior in men and armaments to yours?"

"Castro had every advantage - even the high ground on the bluffs along the roadside - superior numbers, artillery, horses and weaponry. The one advantage that he did not have was fortitude. That one deficiency of his carried the day for us. Our 'bluff' as you put it worked. The evening before battle Castro disbanded his officers and fled, leaving his troops to fend for themselves. It was not long after that the rank and file disbanded and disappeared. The following morning we entered Ciudad Los Angeles, dissolved the Californio Legislature, arrested Governor Pico and a general named Flores. Numerous artillery pieces were discovered and taken as spoils as well as a large number of Castro's officers and men who were now prisoners of war. We had won. California was now a United States Territory."

"An amazing adventure!"

"Do not think for a moment, Grandson that I would not have

followed through on my guarantee to defeat Castro on the field of battle. I was quite prepared to engage the enemy had the ruse not worked. As you see that did not become necessary. Fremont rejoined my main body and we marched into Ciudad Los Angeles unopposed. It was more like a holiday parade than a hard fought battle."

"And all this time I thought that there was more to the California war theater than that."

"There was, and I lay part of the blame squarely on my doorstep. I had been conducting the negotiations between myself and our Mexican prisoners as if we were all gentlemen meeting on the field of battle, that our solemn word was a sacred oath not to be breached. I soon found that not to be the case."

"I don't understand."

"Of course you don't, Robert. I have yet to explain to you what followed. Kindly open your ears and you shall know all."

Sigh.

"I had offered Governor Pico, General Flores and a handful of captured officers amnesty if they would swear on their honor that they would neither take up arms against us nor foment revolt among the Californios. To this they swore and departed to the south toward Sonoma."

"It would be only a few months before I came to know that these men's oaths were of no value." I shall tell you of that shortly but first we must discuss the formation of the Territory government."

"In your use of the word 'discuss' are you implying that we shall have an actual back and forth dialogue or do you mean that in the present context the word means that you will speak and I will listen intently?"

"The latter would be correct, Robert. To continue…. After the victory at Ciudad Los Angeles I immediately drafted a message to President Polk apprising him of the current situation and outlined my plans as Territorial Governor. As there was no significant Californio military activity I then stationed a small garrison of fifty men in Los Angeles under the command of Captain Gillespie and garrisoned Santa Barbara, Monterey and San Francisco with smaller cadres of men. There was peace in California and I believed at the time that no larger forces wwere needed. It was now time to set in place a territorial government with Colonel Fremont as the military governor."

"Why Fremont? You had already appointed yourself as Territorial Governor."

"An excellent question, dear Robert. I had no time to govern as I was busy planning my invasion of Mexico."

CHAPTER ELEVEN

So the Commodore was planning to invade Mexico! I was stunned to hear this latest turn of events in his past life. I knew that we were still at war with Mexico at that historical time but I could never recall any mention of this in anything that I had ever read or heard about the Mexican War. I decided that my best bet was to remain silent for the most part and encourage his retelling of this latest adventure that was about to unfold as we spoke:

"Mexico! How will you do that and maintain the viability of the new California Territory with the very limited number of ground forces available to you?"

"From what I had seen at Mesa and Monterey I held little concern about the Mexican fighters. I was quite certain that a landing by sea at Acapulco would encounter little opposition. Following the taking of that city it was a march of little more than one hundred-eighty-odd miles to Mexico City. I expected little opposition along the way and relished the thought of having coffee with General Zachary Taylor in the Mexican Capitol."

"I am astounded!"

"Yes, well I can tell you that Providence does not always smile

on the aspirations of mere mortals and such was the case for my planned Acapulco landing."

"I'm not sure that I follow. Just what, exactly do you mean?"

"Treachery Grandson, treachery of the most contemptible degree. I had received word from Fremont that the Walla Walla Indian tribe to the north were hostile to our fledgling government and planning an attack. I immediately set sail aboard **Congress** *to investigate this report more fully and if necessary initiate military action against the offenders. Upon my arrival I received word that the Walla Walla Chieftain wished an audience with me. Anticipating the most unfavorable outcome I set in motion the scenario that would allow me to take the Chief captive should the meeting confirm the report of impending attack."*

"An Indian uprising in the north. Do you have enough men to defeat the Walla Wallas if the report is true? I mean it seems to me that your forces are spread awfully thin over a very large piece of geography."

"Fortunately the report was in complete error. I had a quite pleasant meeting with the Walla Walla Chief who confirmed his tribe's loyalty to our new civil government. The Chief further stated that his people were well rid of Castro and his Mexican cutthroats who were both sadistic and brutal in their actions toward his people."

"I'm still not quite clear as to the source of this treachery. Where is the treachery?"

There was a long pause before the Commodore favored me with a reply.

"I suppose that at this stage of our discourse I should have accepted that you are perfectly incapable of allowing me to fully finish my statements regarding the course of events in question. I must say Robert, that there are times when this constant interrupting tries my considerable patience to its very limit."

Hmmm. Time for a 'come to Jesus' meeting.

"Sir, I ask these questions that you see as 'interruptions' to your recollection of events for two reasons: First, I need to slow you down a bit so that I may internalize the conversation for later transcription, and secondly I will be crafting your story in dialogue fashion. This 'interrupting' is necessary for me to properly format our nightly visits. I mean no disrespect I assure you."

"Ah. That is a perfectly acceptable explanation. I shall keep this in mind while we visit. Are you ready to continue?"

"I am, sir."

"The treachery to which I refer came from those very men that I assumed to be gentlemen who kept their word of honor. Once arriving in Sonora, Pico, Jose Flores and an officer named Carillo began recruiting an army of Californios to retake the territory that Castro had lost. Their first objective was to mount an attack on Captain Gillespie's Los Angeles garrison."

"These same men who had sworn on their word of honor not to take up arms again had dishonored themselves and were planning to invade California. I am certain that their motives were purely self serving as they had forfeited much in their defeat of several months earlier."

"Sir, if I may say so it looks to me as if these men do not see this as a duel which is governed by strict rules of engagement. These men view this as all out, anything goes war, just as our country did in 1776. As a famous athlete from my generation once said: 'It ain't over 'till it's over!' These guys are in this to win and are not bound by some archaic code of honor."

"Lamentable, but true. Perhaps I had been acting as if it were an earlier time when officers and gentlemen were bound by their honor. Could it be that I had outlived my usefulness to my country, the country that I had served for more than thirty-eight years?"

Hmmm. Better throttle back a bit here.

"Granddad, let's not dwell on that right now. The battle is about to begin and I'm eager to hear how it went. Let's get back into action."

"It was October of 1846 and I had directed my squadron northward to Yerba Buena. Upon arrival I met with Colonel Fremont and arranged for a celebratory day that would honor the annexation of California. It was while I was there that I received word that an army of Californio rebels had attacked Los Angeles and the garrison of men under Captain Gillespie. The reports were that fighting was fierce and that the garrison was holding, but just barely as food, water and ammunition stores were dangerously low. Twice the rebels had attacked the garrison and twice they had been repelled. The message from Gillespie had also requested reinforcements and provisions. Sensing the immediacy of the situation I directed Captain Mervine commanding the ***Savannah*** *and an accompanying stores vessel to embark a force of marines and proceed south to San Pedro where he was to land and proceed inland and relieve the Los Angeles garrison."*

"And so the rebellion begins. Am I to assume that Mervine landed his men and proceeded to relieve and resupply the L.A. - I mean Los Angeles garrison?"

"Assume what you wish, Grandson. The facts surrounding the battle was that after repulsing the enemy several times and exhibiting great fortitude and skill the opposing force was too great to overcome and Gillespie, along with the remaining garrison and Mervine's relief force were forced out and fled to safety at San Pedro."

"Wow. After thirty-eight years you suffer your first defeat. If you were to ask me I think that's a pretty good record. My guess is that you were not about to let this battle go unchallenged."

"The reality of the situation was that we were faced with a superior force. The Californios were superb horsemen having spent their entire lives on horseback. Their mounted lancers were the equal of the finest European cavalry. They were well trained and well armed and had canvassed the countryside for all available horses, mules, cattle and sheep. The American southern forces were without these vital necesseties and the countryside could provide nothing to remedy the situation, having been swept clean by the Californios."

"While Mervine's reinforcements were en route to Los Angeles I met with Colonel Fremont and directed him to raise a force of one thousand American volunteers from the American population in the north and to scour the countryside for horses, beasts of labor, cattle and sheep and when he had finished training this force to proceed southward and join me at San Pedro where I would have already taken the harbor to use as a repositioning area. From there my plan was to proceed to Los Angeles and retake the village, garrison it and move southward toward San Diego, thus securing

the southern part of the territory and driving the rebels back into Mexico."

"Well then with fresh troops and horses and so forth I guess the village was retaken once Fremont's reinforcements arrived."

"We are getting a bit ahead of ourselves here, Robert. I wish to take you back to mid October of that year. **Congress** *was badly in need of a refit and as the situation was calm and under our control I laid her up and dismantled her spars and rigging and set the carpenters to work on an overhaul. When the report of the attack to the south reached me I gave orders to have* **Congress** *ready for sea within forty-eight hours. Spars and rigging had to be replaced, cannonry re-mounted, ammunition and stores onloaded and a force of three hundred embarked."*

Now was no time to interrupt Granddad. I kept my mouth shut and waited for him to continue.

"Landing at San Pedro several days hence I was met by the remnants of Gillespie's and Mervine's forces and began to set our perimeter defenses. It wasn't long before Flores tested us with an assault by his forces which were superior in number to mine. The assault was beaten back causing a number of enemy casualties. The rebels had their noses bloodied in the assault and adopted a strategy of harassment and sniping designed to demoralize our troops. When I would send out a scouting party it would be set upon by Flores' men and when our larger force was sent to extricate them the rebels would fall back in the hills and cointinue their harassing fire. This continued for several weeks, frustrating our efforts to join up with Fremont, whom I had directed to land at Santa Barbara and procure horses there for his men. Once joined we would proceed to Los Angeles and attack Flores' forces."

"Sounds good to me, unless there's a Murphy here somewhere."

"Murphy? Who in God's name is Murphy? What does this 'Murphy' have to do with this?"

"Oh, sorry. I was referring to a modern term known as 'Murphy's Law' which states that if something can go wrong, it will."

"Hah. Murphy's Law. I shall have quite an interesting vocabulary after visiting with you these past few times."

"Unfortunately this Mr. Murphy is correct. I had directed Colonel Fremont to land at Santa Barbara and retake the garrison that was abandoned when Flores and his rebels took Los Angeles. Fremont's orders were to retake the garrison and marshal all quadripeds for use as mounted cavalry and transport. After scouring the countryside his men could find no horses. He then opted to proceed north to Monterey ***some five hundred-odd miles to the north*** *to locate cavalry mounts!"*

"Not good, sir. Does this mean your assault on Los Angeles failed?"

"It does not, sir. I did, however reassess the current situation and determined that my forces were at a disadvantage. We had no horses with which to confront the Californio lancers and we were faced with an opposing force that was superior in both numbers and armaments. What is more the winter storm season was rapidly approaching making the San Pedro harborage untenable. It was time for a new strategy. I would redeploy my naval units and foot

brigade south to the protected harbor of San Diego where I would mount an assault from the south."

"Did Fremont ever manage to join the battle?"

"All in good time, Robert. Please allow me to finish presenting the situation as existed at the time of our arrival in San Diego.

"Certainly. Please continue."

"By the time of our San Diego arrival my force was extremely low on supplies. I had the men suffer reduced rations in order to preserve our stores as long as possible. I was extremely dismayed to find that the San Diego garrison was also in extremis, their provisions were dangerously low and the garrison was literally surrounded on three sides by Major General Pico's Californios."

"Surrounded or no the facts of the situation were that we desperately required food and horses. I despatched a party southward to Lower California to forage. While they eventually succeeded it was nearly one month hence until their arrival in camp with a sufficient quantity of horses and cattle. Meanwhile I had set the men to crafting cannon carriages for the coming battle and set about drilling the men in formations that would confound a successful method of attack."

"Interesting. What were the rebels using that was so successful?"

"The rebels had many horses, both mounted and wild. They would direct a stampede of wild horses toward our infantry rank and when the stampede broke the formation the mounted lancers would

simply charge through the broken ranks and attack, often with great success."

"Okay. That seems like a working strategy. How did you defeat it?"

"I began having the army shift rapidly from an advance line to a formation of squares, each square being four ranks deep. When the stampede would charge the first rank would fire a volley of musket fire then kneel on one knee and fix the butt of their muskets firmly on the ground with the bayonets pointing upward at a sixty-five degree angle. Horses are not dumb creatures, Grandson. They will not charge barriers. They will simply turn off to either side leaving the enemy's mounted cavalry exposed to withering musket volleys from the succeeding inner ranks."

"Nice. And this tactic carried the day when you attacked Los Angeles?"

The Commodore's blood was up. I could sense his excitement. He was fighting the California battle once again.

"Once again we have strayed a bit ahead, no doubt due to my exuberance. Let me introduce Brigadier General Kearny into the narrative."

"Kearny? What happened to Fremont?"

"Fremont was a man cut from the same cloth as I. While I had not yet received word of his whereabouts I knew that he was headed south to join the gathering battle."

"Now then, about Kearny. Kearny had left Fort Leavenworth

some months earlier with his brigade of Dragoons. His orders were to bring the war to New Mexico, defeat any opposition there and annex it as a United States Territory. Once accomplished his orders further directed him to proceed to California, defeat the rebels in battle and establish a civil government."

"Wait! You have already done this. There is a territorial government already in place and Fremont is the Governor."

"Kearny's orders, like mine were old and out of date. In short, my actions earlier had made his instructions moot. I use that term advisedly as Kearny and I would have more than one - let us say discussion - on the issue of command after his arrival."

"I digress. On to the circumstances surrounding his arrival."

"An advance scout from Kearny's army reached me in early December to inform me of his impending arrival. After subduing the enemy in New Mexico Kearny directed much of his brigade back to Leavenworth and continued ahead with some eighty dragoons. They had endured much hardship in crossing the Sierra Nevada Mountains. Many of his dragoons were forced to mount mules as horses were in short supply. Upon learning of his situation I despatched Captain Gillespie with some forty-odd men and a cannon to meet up with Kearny's army and guide them to our San Diego garrison."

"Kearny's arrival will make the Los Angeles attack all that easier won't it?"

"Kearny had trouble of his own. Upon the arrival of Captain Gillespie and his troop Kearny decided upon a surprise attack on a force of Californios at San Pasquale led by Don Pico that

Gillespie had detected on his journey inland. Kearny coveted the Californio horses and sent a scout party out to locate the exact enemy position. It was apparent that the scouts were deficient in their understanding of the word stealth and were detected by an enemy patrol."

I could hear the disapproval in Granddad's voice. I was soon to understand why.

"In a desperate move - one with which I disagree may I add - Kearny ordered his men to attack at midnight. The night was cold and wet, as were Kearny's men and powder. To compound the developing disaster there was confusion among the officers as to exactly when to order the charge. After an intense battle often necessitating hand to hand fighting Kearny's force was beaten back. Kearny himself was wounded as was Captain Gillespie. The Americans took a defensive position on a Godforsaken location known as Mule Hill. They had no food or water and very little ammunition. It was a dire predicament for Kearny and his men."

"The General was between a rock and a hard place. From your earlier remarks I gather that he somehow escaped."

"Desperate for relief, Kearny despatched Kit Carson to San Diego to assess me of his perilous position. Upon learning of his misfortune I began to prepare to move my entire army to relieve him."

"He'll be quite happy to get a visit from the U.S. Navy that far inland."

"Ha-ha. I'm certain of it. Before departing I deployed scouts to determine the enemy's strength overland to Mule Hill. The report came back that we were facing a force of no more than one hundred

men. I then decided that a faster force of no more than twice that amount would suffice. Time was of the essence as Kearny's position was untenable. He had to be extricated from his situation as quickly as possible. Once Kearny had safely reached San Diego we could begin preparations for the Los Angeles campaign and while doing so sort out the issues of overall command."

"Issues? What issues?"

"It pains me to think that a fellow Jerseyman would take such underhanded measures to subvert my actions in California. Let me elaborate: You should first know that Kit Carson was my scout and not Kearny's. In August I had despatched Carson with an express communication to the President in Washington to the effect that California had been conquered and the Californio and Mexican army under Castro had been defeated. I further informed Mr. Polk that I had established a civil government over the Territory and that I was the Territorial Governor and Commander-in-Chief of American forces west of the Sierra Madres."

"On his express journey eastward Carson came upon General Kearny and his brigade of one thousand dragoons. For reasons that still remain a mystery to me Carson divulged the contents of the communication to Kearny, who then directed all but eighty of his force to return to Leavenworth and pressed Carson into service to lead his much reduced force westward to our San Diego garrison."

"What? Do you mean that Kearny intercepted your message to the President and kept it? How can that not be a court martial offense?"

"The man's deviousness knew no bounds. He did not destroy

the letter but merely sent one of his own officers to Washington with the missive. Had Carson managed to carry out his orders much unpleasantness could have been avoided several months hence as Carson would have no doubt returned with fresh orders acknowledging the fact of the defeat of Castro and the establishment of a Territorial government. Kearny could then have returned to Leavenworth where he belonged."

"I can see that you are not a happy camper regarding this turn of events."

"Happy camper? I will assume that you have burdened me with another of your modern metaphors. No matter. Let us move forward."

"Kearny and his small party were more trouble than they were worth. While they did participate in quelling the uprising in Los Angeles you can be assured that our brave sailors and marines carried the day when the battle was at hand."

"Once we had safely escorted the remnants of Kearny's force I gave orders to begin preparation for the assault on the rebels in Los Angeles. I then offered command of our assault forces to General Kearny and offered to accompany him as his aide. Kearny declined this most generous offer, not once but several times in the presence of witnesses." He then offered to act in subordinate position to me for the advance and attack on Los Angeles."

"I'm not sure that I understand the man's motives, although I'm sure that you are wary of him by this time."

"All too true I am sad to report. First, however we shall discuss the battle to defeat the insurgents once and for all."

"I can hear the excitement in your voice. God I wish I'd been there with you."

"Well, Grandson relax in that contraption that you always occupy and I will take you there. Close your eyes, clear your head and concentrate. We are about to show the Californios the resolve of the American fighting man."

"Our forces numbered about five hundred-fifty men of which Kearny's decimated brigade represented only about ten percent. They had been badly mauled at San Pasqual and to be quite candid I held little faith in their ability to engage the enemy. Our forces were divided into mounted cavalry riflemen, infantry musketeers and infantry carbineers. The foot soldiers, sailors and marines would move forward in files and ranks and when attacked by the enemy lancers the musketeers would shift upon command into the square formations to repel the horsemen's advance and allow our mounted dragoons to penetrate to the inner infantry."

It was the oddest thing. I could actually see the troops moving toward the battlefield. The infantry was haphazardly dressed in anything that could be scavenged and shod in hastily cobbled shoes with muskets at 'carry arms'. The choking dust and noise from the horses and wagons traveling over the rough trail was so intense that my breathing became labored as we moved forward. I could hear the officers shouting encouragement to the infantry, constantly moving up and down the advancing line. The cheers and hurrahs of the ranks were overwhelming. I thought to myself that the energy and noise of our force alone would be enough to break the will of the waiting enemy.

The Americans were eager for battle!

"As we approached San Luis Rey I received a communication from Kearny stating his desire to be relieved from command of the ground forces. I was somewhat taken aback with this and summoned Lieutenant Rowan, an able marine officer and charged him with commanding the ground force during the battle about to unfold."

My reverie was interrupted.

"What is the man up to? His behavior sounds to me like he's just plain unstable."

"No sir, he was anything but unstable. Kearny may have believed that the sailors and marines were not likely to defeat a trained ground force and wished to remove himself from all culpability in case of an American defeat."

"No sir, he was not unstable. He was in my opinion a self serving and cunning man whose only desire was the governorship of California. I found it extremely distasteful to have interaction with him but when necessary I showed him the utmost courtesy and deference - as a senior would show someone equal in rank but lower in standing."

"Keep your friends close and your enemies closer, eh Granddad?"

"Yes sir. That is the objective."

"Our force was equal in numbers to that of the enemy but inferior to them in supply and weaponry. We were, however, spoiling for a fight and I had hoped to rendezvous with Fremont's force at San Luis Rey."

"Our force, short of supply and ammunition had nevertheless made progress toward Ciudad Los Angeles when what should appear on the horizon but an enemy scout party bearing a flag of truce. I gave the order to Lieutenant Rowan to despatch a small cadre to escort the rebels to me as I was curious to know to what mischief they aspired. This was done to my satisfaction and I addressed the officer in charge of the enemy scout party in the most demeaning terms that I could muster"

"My guess is that they wanted to gather intelligence on the strength of your army."

"You are correct for the most part. The enemy officer delivered to me a missive from Flores suggesting a truce while both armies sent emissaries to Washington and Mexico City to determine if the war had been concluded. He had the effrontery to sign the letter as "Commander-in-Chief and Governor General of California."

"I am unable to accurately describe to you the outrage that I felt upon seeing this criminal's name affixed to the title that he had given himself. I took the letter and threw it back in the rebel officer's face and proceeded to dictate to him a counter offer."

I couldn't wait to hear the response.

"I informed the rebel officer that I would consider nothing less than unconditional surrender of his forces and that the liar and scoundrel Flores be turned over to me to be placed before a firing squad."

Vintage Commodore! Inferior in weapons and supply, the men worn to near exhaustion and facing an enemy who had taken the high ground for the coming battle but not giving an inch! The man had a backbone of pure steel.

"The rebel then made an attempt to appeal to my good nature by stating that the civilian populace would suffer greatly if our two armies were to engage in this 'mighty clash' of arms. I then proposed a second offer. His army would surrender their arms and all cannonry, horses and supplies to me and go peacefully to their homes and families. I would in turn guarantee their safety and rights as territorial citizens of the United States."

"And Flores? What about Flores?"

"The dishonorable liar would still be handed over to face a firing squad."

"Well your bluff did work earlier with Castro. Did Flores face a firing squad?"

"No. The rebel officer and his party returned to relay my counter proposal and no more was heard of it."

"I sense a battle looming in the near future."

"Indeed. We would face the rebel on their terms."

"I'm not sure I understand what you mean."

"We were encamped on the southern bank of the Rio San Gabriel, a shallow and muddy bottomed river. On the north side Flores and his rebels were entrenched both on the far bank and in the cliffs overlooking the river. As we prepared for battle I was greeted by General Kearny who had apparently thought better of his former request and asked me as Commander-in-Chief would I reinstate

him as commander of the ground forces. Exhibiting the utmost deference and courtesy to him I summoned Lieutenant Rowan and repeated the General's request. To his credit, Rowan was most gracious and acceded to the General's desire. Kearny was back in the fray for better or for worse."

"What were Kearny's motives for this 'flip flop' if you will?"

"I have given up trying to make sense of your modern euphemisms however I believe that I understand your question. I think that Kearny was concerned as to how his standing would appear if the battle were won with himself effectively in the rear while a Lieutenant commanded the tactical ground forces."

"Let us continue. As we drew near the south bank of the San Gabriel the rebel artillery began shelling us from the heights with little effect. We began to ford the river, artillery pieces being the first to attempt the river crossing."

My eyes were again closed and I concentrated on Granddad's voice. It was deep and commanding.

"As we began to ford the river the mules and artillery pieces became mired in the mud and soft sand of the river. Enemy shells were bursting all around but had little effect on our force. I remember thinking that the enemy gunners could use some advice from my sailor and marine gunners. The rebels were sending many shells toward our force which was beginning to bog down in the mud but miraculously they scored no direct hits nor did they inflict any casualties."

"I could see that the mules that were pulling the artillery pieces were becoming disoriented by the exploding artillery and shouts of the

artillerymen and as mules have done since time immemorial they halted and refused to go any further. Lieutenant Tilghman who was commanding the artillery approached me to apprise me of the situation, which I could readily see with my own eyes. I mounted one of the pack mules on the south bank and rode into water that was waist deep. Man and mule alike were in a state of panic and confusion. It was time to lead the charge. I leaped from the mule, turned to the men and shouted in a commanding tone, **'COME ON MEN, FOLLOW YOUR COMMODORE'** *and began the crossing determined to be the first to set foot on the opposite bank. At this time I received a messenger from Kearny suggesting I withdraw and allow the infantry to ford first. I told the messenger that by the time my reply reached him my artillery would be on the opposite bank. I asked the messenger for Kearny's location on the south bank, the fellow pointing to a position only twenty or so yards to the east. I signaled the General to begin his crossing and to his credit he was soon by my side leading our forces into the teeth of the enemy's formation."*

"After much pulling and coaxing the mules began to move and our artillery men and pieces reached the north bank. I then directed that the cannon be unmasked and prepared for firing. I personally aimed the first piece and gave the order to fire, scoring a direct hit on an enemy cannon on the heights! Kearny's troops had by this time reached the north bank and began to move inland, Flores countering with his wild stallion stampede which of course was well known to us by this time. The General ordered the rank to assume 'fours' and thus repelled the charge, inflicting casualties on both the horses and the lancers following the stampede.

It was as if I were somehow above the battlefield. The scene was crystal clear to me: The screams of the dead and wounded men and the dying sounds of the horses wild eyed with terror was near to overwhelming. It was as if I were alongside the Commodore himself advancing into the teeth of the enemy army. The smoke and dust from the battle was choking, the smell of gunpowder and the sound of the artillery pieces and small arms was everywhere.

Above all the noise and confusion came The Commodore's voice, shouting commands and urging his men on to victory.

"STEADY BOYS, STEADY. DON'T MISS A SHOT. I'M CHOCK FULL OF FIGHT. ANDY JACKSON! ANDY JACKSON! WE'LL SEND THESE REBELS BACK TO MEXICO WITH THEIR TAILS BETWEEN THEIR REBEL LEGS!"

Three times the Californios charged and were met with musket fire and the cold steel of our bayonets and three times they fell back. Finally the Californio army withdrew, taking their dead and wounded with them. The Commodore and the General and their ragtag army, short on provisions and ammunition but long on heart and fighting spirit were victorious.

"What about casualties? Did we pay a heavy price for the victory? And what about the rebels? How many of the enemy were lost?"

"Two of our brave lads fell in battle and nine more received wounds of varying severity. As for the rebels I can only speculate as they took their dead and wounded form the field when they retired. My officers estimated that more than fifty casualties were inflicted on the rebel force."

"A clear cut victory for your army which I suppose provided a clear path to Los Angeles."

"The rebels had halted their withdrawal after six miles at another high ground location known to the Californios as Mesa. It was there that Flores was determined to make his stand and it was there that the final battle of the insurrection was fought."

I closed my eyes and applied a death grip to the arms of the recliner. I was as excited and apprehensive as I had ever been. The adrenaline was really flowing.

"It was the morning of January ninth. We were advancing toward the seat of the rebel government in Los Angeles when we began receiving a tremendous artillery barrage from cannon that Flores had placed in a small ravine on our left flank. I ordered our artillery to be unmasked and to return fire. ***FIRE AT WILL, BOYS! MAKE EVERY VOLLEY COUNT!"***

The roar of the artillery pieces was deafening. The old Commodore was directing the counter battery fire personally and with incredible accuracy! Then came the shouts of the rebel cavalry as they charged Kearny's mix and match infantry.

"The rebel cavalry had changed their tactics from the previous day. When Kearny ordered his infantry to form 'fours' in order to counter the cavalry charge the rebel Flores ordered his mounted lancers to wheel and attack all four sides of the square simultaneously. The engagement was bloody and for a time I felt the outcome may be in doubt. I then ordered one of our cannon to be loaded with grapeshot, turned upon the rebel attack and personally aimed and fired, causing many rebel casualties. This was the final blow to the

rebel army, which then retreated helter skelter toward Los Angeles with Kearny's troops in hot pursuit."

"Once again the field of battle was ours."

The battle and presumably the insurrection was over. I was exhausted, gasping for breath.

"I don't understand it but somehow I was right there alongside you in the thick of the battle. What an experience!"

"Ha-ha. I thought that a bit of first hand knowledge would assist you in writing the narrative. Did you enjoy yourself?"

"I don't think that the term 'enjoy yourself' quite covers the range of emotions that I experienced while I was at your side. By the way that was pretty fair aiming when you let go with that load of grapeshot."

"Ha-ha. Yes indeed it certainly carried the day, although I'm convinced that General Kearny may not share your opinion."

"Well it seems to me that Flores and his army is pretty much done for. Was there a final battle to be fought?"

"We advanced to within three miles of Ciudad Los Angeles and encamped for the night. I began to plan for the final push into the village when an emissary from the rebel camp approached under the protection of a white flag. The rebels offered to disband and leave the village if we would guarantee the safety of its citizens and property. My response to this offer was to provide the guarantee provided they hand over General Flores to me to face a firing squad."

"Which, of course they refused to do."

"The emissary informed me that Flores and a band of rebels had fled to Mexico soon after the Mesa battle and was no longer in command of the rebel army."

"Suspecting treachery I bid the emissary wait whilst I conferred with General Kearny. We were both in agreement that we would accept the terms of the remaining rebel force but would enter the village in battle formation to prevent a surprise encounter. I held little faith in the word of a rebel."

"Well? Do we fight again?"

"The insurrection was finished. We marched into Ciudad de Los Angeles unopposed and I began to set up the necessary arrangements to restore the civil government that was in place before the rebel Flores interfered."

"I have heard nothing about Colonel Fremont in all this. What happened to him?"

"Fremont! I was much displeased with Colonel Fremont's actions when he met up with Don Pico's forces to the north at Cahuenga. The Colonel had no information regarding the victories of my army in the south when he moved south with his northern army of four hundred men. On the twelfth he encountered General Pico's northern force. Pico had been appointed Commander-in-Chief of the rebels when Flores turned tail and ran. Pico sent his emissary to Colonel Fremont offering to unconditionally surrender if Fremont would grant amnesty to his men and himself along with the others who had broken their parole to fight. Fremont, as I have previously

said knew nothing of the success of our southern army agreed and ***accepted Pico's sword in surrender!"***

You could have heard that last part three states away. The Commodore was livid at the unilateral action taken by Fremont.

"You sound upset and I don't for the life of me know why. Pico's surrender eliminates the last elements of resistance to your territorial claim. California was now a sovereign territory of the United States, you are Commander-in-Chief of all U.S. forces in the Territory and the Territorial governor. Why the anger at Fremont?"

"The signing of a peace treaty with the enemy and the acceptance of their leader's sword is the sole prerogative of the Commander-in Chief and Governor. Fremont had embarrassed me by presenting me with a fait accompli. There was nothing that I could do no other than ratify the treaty which Fremont had negotiated and signed."

"Forgive me sir but I'm still not quite clear as to exactly why you were upset with Fremont. Would you not have dictated essentially the same terms?"

The Commodore heaved an exasperated sigh.

"Let me attempt to clarify once again: Included in Fremont's amnesty were the insurrectionists and parole breakers that had disavowed their oath not to take up arms. In my earlier peace terms to the rebels ***I had granted amnesty to all but the parole breakers.*** *Those men were to have been turned over to the army and made prisoners.* ***That,*** *Grandson is specifically why I was not*

pleased with Fremont's actions. I would never have agreed to allow those scoundrels to go free."

And all discussion on the subject was finished. Period.

"My intentions were to appoint Colonel Fremont as Territorial Governor and return to **Congress** *in San Diego to plan for our invasion of Mexico. It was at this time that I received a letter from Kearny demanding - yes, demanding - to know by what authority did I appoint Fremont to that position when he had direct orders from the President to establish the California Territorial government."*

"This sounds to me like the beginning of what I would call a 'pissing contest' to see who's really in charge."

"Your impertinent remarks do nothing to address the importance of the issues at hand and will be ignored by me from this point forward."

"My response to this insult from Kearny was to remind him that his orders stated that he was specifically directed to 'conquer the Californios and Mexicans and establish a government.' Both of these objectives had already been accomplished before his arrival."

The Commodore was really agitated. I decided that it was time to keep my mouth shut and let him continue.

"Kearny shot back that when he arrived in the territory there was insurrection and war, thus his orders were on point and operative. I replied that having heard from Kit Carson that I had vanquished Castro and established a civil government he foolishly sent more than eight hundred of his force back to Leavenworth leaving him

less than one hundred men with which to face a vastly superior force. I also stated that this action demonstrated his tacit agreement that a government was already in place albeit having to confront an ongoing insurrection. I also reminded Kearny that it was my army that rescued his pathetically small force at San Pasqual and that had I not done so his small band would all have been killed or captured."

"Kearny would have had to learn Spanish the hard way."

I couldn't help myself.

"I had learned through an intermediary that the General had briefly contemplated civil war to assert his claim but had discarded the idea after he was reminded of the reduced state of his small force of dragoons. He then journeyed to San Diego, embarked aboard **Cyane** *with his remaining force and proceeded to Monterey to await further orders from Washington."*

"By this time Colonel Fremont had learned of Kearny's attempt to block him from assuming the position of Territorial Governor and had replied that he was bound to follow my orders and directives as he found a governing body in place when he had first arrived in Monterey some months earlier and then assumed the duties of the office, issuing a proclamation of peace."

"And that didn't sit well with Kearny, did it?"

"It would eventually lead to a humiliating court martial of Colonel Fremont by the Army for failing to obey his senior officer and mutiny. Fremont, were it not for the influence he possessed in Washington could well have received the death penalty."

"I have to know....what was the outcome of the court-martial?"

"Despite testimony from those present in California during the suppression of the insurrection including testimony from me Fremont was found guilty, stripped of his rank and cashiered from the Army."

"That doesn't seem to square with the facts as you have presented them to me."

"No it does not 'square' as you put it at all. You will be pleased to know that President Polk shared your opinion of the verdict and pardoned Colonel Fremont, offering to restore him to his former rank. Fremont, being a man of honor declined and left the Army."

"And Kearny? What became of Kearny?"

"Kearny! The man was extremely apprehensive as to the direction that my testimony would lead and approached me via an intermediary wishing to effect a rapprochement as to our California difficulties. He offered to testify that it was I who led the combined forces that conquered the California Territory and not he. In return I gave my word that I would not divulge the man's constant attempts to usurp my authority and take credit as the commander of the forces."

"After the trial Kearny was promoted to Major General and sent to Mexico where he contracted yellow fever. He returned to St. Louis where he died two years thereafter."

"Now I suppose that we go on to your invasion of the west coast of Mexico."

My remark was met with a long and ominous pause. Finally the Commodore spoke:

"There was to be no assault on Acapulco. On the 23rd of January of the Year of Our Lord 1847 Captain William Shubrick arrived in Monterey with orders from the President to invest the office of Territorial Governor in General Kearny. Further, as Shubrick was my senior in time in rank the title of Commodore and commander of the Pacific Squadron fell upon his ancient and withered shoulders. Shubrick was the officer who conducted the investigation subsequent to the Peacemaker explosion. There was no love lost between us, however orders are given to be obeyed."

"I can't believe it! Has anyone in Washington read any of your messages regarding the California war?"

"I must tell you in all candor that the bold actions taken by me troughout my naval service to my country had made many enemies among both my peers and seniors. I of course cared not a fig for any of their disparagements nor do I even today. As I have said many times during our visits Nelson's 'creative disobedience' is a two edged sword. Fortunately throughout the years following the 1812 war with the British I was well positioned in Washington to withstand the repercussions that men like Shubrick, Biddle and others wished to use to hold me in check. Beginning with the events in Texas and later the controversy surrounding the governorship of the California Territory was, I must tell you, the beginning of the final chapter of my naval service to these great United States."

"What exactly did Shubrick do after his arrival at Monterey?"

"Upon his arrival I crafted a letter to Shubrick requesting that I be retained in my offices until definitive word arrived from Washington regarding the muddle that Kearny had caused. Shubrick did not afford me the courtesy of a reply and so in several days time I had transited from Commander-in-Chief of the United States California forces and Governor General of California to that of a mere Captain commanding the frigate **Congress**. *Then to worsen matters Commodore Biddle arrived in Monterey and replaced Shubrick."*

"Is that the same Biddle that you butted heads with in the West Indies?"

"Indeed. One and the same."

I had the sense that the mission which brought us together over the past ten days was about to end.

"I doubt that Biddle would return you to your previous position."

"I had written Biddle essentially the same letter that I had Shubrick along with the reminder that his brother Nicholas had been a business partner of mine for many years and had prospered. My request was once again to maintain status quo until a more definitive word arrived from Washington. My thoughts were that after Washington had read the accounting of Kearny's divisive actions that a reversal was sure to occur. I also stated in the letter my observation that the whole business smelled of the Army - which by the way had powerful allies in Congress and the Cabinet - was

attempting to wrest the glory from the Navy and rob her of her rightful place in the history of the California conquest."

"And? What did Biddle do?"

"For the first time in his naval career he made a decision without waiting for word from afar. He denied my request. I realized that there was no hope of my return to office and began to make plans for my return home."

"And that, Grandson is where I must leave you for now. I had wanted to tell you of my adventure traveling home overland with Kit Carson and a scrofulous band of cutthroats, frenchy trappers and Indian fighters but my time allotted is finished and I must take leave."

"There is so much more that I want to know, your time in Congress as a Senator, your Presidential aspirations, all that you had mentioned on our first visit."

"Robert, there have been many so-called 'historians' that have rewritten and revised the facts surrounding my conquest of California. I am giving you the charge of righting those libelous historical wrongs. You have been privy to my first hand accounting of events as they happened over time. This is the task that I wish for you to undertake and all that I am allowed to reveal through this bizarre medium. Perhaps we can reconnect at a later time to discuss my further adventures."

"Well sir, I am certainly not looking forward to a 'bizarre medium' that requires both broken bones and heavy sedation. I hope that we do meet again under less 'bizarre' circumstances."

"Yes. Goodbye, Grandson and God speed you on your mission."

I awoke and looked at the cable box clock. It was four o'clock in the morning and my right side was really barking. The room was cold, dark and empty.

I eased up out of the damned recliner and headed for the kitchen.